STRUCTURING THE CLASSROOM SUCCESSFULLY FOR

COOPERATIVE TEAM LEARNING

Teresa L. Cantlon

Prestige Publishers
Portland, Oregon

Cantlon, Teresa L.
    Structuring the Classroom Successfully For
    Cooperative Team Learning

    Bibliography for Educators
    Author's Glossary of Terms and Index

LB89-090813
ISBN -0-9622312-0-7

$24

Prestige   Publishers
P.O. Box 19044
Portland, Oregon 97219
503/588-0222   or   503/694-5970

Cover photography: Wayne Gooding

Third edition
Printed and bound in the United States of America

This book is written for educators new to cooperative learning, those using cooperative learning but experiencing some drawbacks, and for supervisors of teachers using cooperative learning strategies.

Section ten is designed for those who support, supervise, or evaluate teachers using these strategies.

This book is designed to be used as a resource. It is formatted step-by-step on **how** *to* structure your classroom, **what** to incorporate, and **what** to avoid to be successful with this teaching technique.

Some "points" or strategies resurface throughout the book. This is done intentionally. If a reader needs to review or reads this book by "sections" the points of emphasis are included in each section.

There are "NOTES" sections throughout this book, please use them to jot down ideas.

Many thanks to the hundreds of teachers I have trained who invite me into their classrooms or send me videotapes to critique and give them feedback.

It is through these observations, training, and my own experiences that I have developed this book.

For all those educators who believe that...

"Cooperatively, we can do together,
what many of us can NOT do alone..."

Good luck!
Teresa Cantlon

As an Elementary Teacher:

When Teresa's colleagues had their students' desks in rows, her students were side-by-side assisting and "teaching" one another.

As a High School Teacher:

Teaching labeled "At Risk" students; she removed their traditional desks and replaced them with round tables. Student attendance improved and a "little" student effort was being rewarded through positive "feedback" from their teacher and interaction with peers.

As a Special Education Teacher:

Students were "teamed" as partners and responsible for one another's skills (academic and social). These students' annual academic achievement ranged from a minimum 1.5 years to 2.5 years gain.

As an Elementary Principal:

A building goal was to incorporate cooperative learning strategies. Changes in student attitudes about themselves and others began surfacing. The "have not" students felt comfortable joining into any group or game on the playground. Students who normally did not interact with one another were becoming friends.

Schoolwide discipline problems were lowered due to students acquiring skills to solve their conflicts. Naturally academic achievement is not far behind with raised self esteem, new friendships and learning how to set positive goals.

As a Full Time Trainer and Consultant:

Teresa now trains educators nationally, on How to Structure Their Classrooms Successfully for Cooperative Team Learning.

She is in the classroom weekly, in all parts of the nation, modelling lessons, observing teachers and giving feedback.

Teachers are welcome to send her videos of their cooperative lessons for feedback toward improvement.

It is through her own lifelong experiences, training, and observations of hundreds of teachers' cooperative learning lessons that she has developed her philosophy and techniques on what makes Cooperative Team Learning work **successfully**.

Train with Teresa in Cooperative Team Learning Strategies and Classroom Management Techniques. One, two, or four day training. Summer Institutes can be brought to your district or train in Oregon.
    For information and national references call or write:

C&M Education Consultants
P.O. Box 19044
Portland, Oregon 97219
(503) 588-0222 or (503) 694-5970

NOTE: Some concepts and strategies resurface in several "Sections." This book is formatted to be read in its entirety or by Sections of interest. Therefore, concepts are reviewed in applicable Sections for reinforcement.

TABLE OF CONTENTS

Table of Contents - continued

WHAT IS... COOPERATIVE TEAM LEARNING?

Section 1

"It's the shot in the arm my teaching needed,"..."I feel I can return to my classroom with a new 'tool' to reach my students"... "My students are excited again about school and learning."

Teachers across the nation are making statements similar to these. What is it that is putting the "zip" into the teachers' attitudes and is building self esteem and raising academic achievement in classrooms?

It is **Cooperative Team Learning,** a teaching strategy which educators put aside several decades ago when they decided to use individualized techniques to reach our youth.

We have since discovered individualized learning is the least effective learning technique. By learning and being taught solely in an individualized or competitive format we are sending our students out to seek jobs only to lose them because companies require their employees to work in a cooperative, team-oriented structure with *goal-setting objectives.*

Cooperative Team Learning is a learning strategy in which students work as small teams to accomplish set tasks or goals.

These tasks can be in **any** of the subject areas and include the teaching or review of appropriate *social skills.*

Ten to twenty-five per cent of the students in any classroom have **few or no friends.** They do not have appropriate social skills necessary to get along with others. Therefore, in-classroom modeling and application of these much needed social skills are a part of a teacher's lesson.

It works this way: The teams will be together for an extended period of time (for example, two weeks to a month) and find that, if they are successful in reaching their goals (not only with their academic task, but with their partner(s)while working together), they will receive *various rewards* .

The rewards can include: raising their grade, bonus points toward a privilege, free time, stickers, stamps, certificates, praise, etc., whatever is appropriate for the needs and levels of the students.

However, once cooperative strategies are in place, commonly, the biggest reward is the satisfaction of a job well done because:

" Cooperatively we can do together, what many of us can NOT do alone."
-Teresa Cantlon

Why have Cooperative Team Learning?
Because it is realistic.

"Our world is not a dog-eat-dog world. It is a person helping world. Almost all human activity is cooperative, from our common language to our sets of laws governing our actions, to our economic system characterized by an elaborate division of labor." -Johnson & Johnson

We live in families and communities held together by our common interests and goals.

Corporations today are looking for employees who can work as a team. Why not train our students to be successful in the real world?

Cooperative Team Learning is not new. It is an instructional technique which has been around for decades and is NOT the sole technique used in a classroom.

Classrooms in which Cooperative Team Learning is used also employ **individual** tasks as well as **whole class instruction**.

Research supports the concept that cooperative learning is beneficial to **ALL** students. In terms of motivation and actual achievement, the largest gainers are the struggling low-achieving students, and the next largest gainers are the middle-achieving students.

High-achieving students using Cooperative Learning score higher on retention tests than do high-achieving students participating in competitive or individualistic learning situations.

The cognitive processes involved in having to talk through and explain the material enhances retention and promotes higher-level reasoning strategies. High-achieving students also benefit from the development of social skills and friendships.

But, more importantly, studies show
We LEARN:
  10% of what we **read**
  20% of what we **hear**
  30% of what we see
  50% of what we both **see and hear**
And:
  70% of what is **discussed** with others
  80% of what we **experience** personally
  95% of what we TEACH someone else
  -Wm Glasser

Students learn best when given the opportunity to share their ideas, opinions, how they learn, and how they might apply what they are learning to life skills, **aloud**.

In addition, they are more likely to develop the leadership, communication, decision-making, and conflict management skills they need for future career and family success.

Cooperative Team Learning helps all students to learn not only academics, but positive social skills, teaching them to be more caring people who are willing to help others.

And Cooperative Team Learning is fun, too...Each lesson has specific steps to be followed:

First, the teams are reminded of- and review with the teacher, the **Ground Rules**. Ground Rules are three or four basic observable teachable behaviors which initially assist teams to function appropriately, while working.

The materials are assembled, often limited or shared (to draw the teammembers closer), and the objective of the lesson is discussed.

If appropriate or necessary, roles are assigned. With small teams, the Ground Rule of Take Turns is usually enough to keep everyone actively involved throughout the lesson.

So that each team is successful, goals that can be accomplished are set. These goals may be: getting seven out of ten questions correct, or receiving three positive tallies on their assignment or Team Card from the teacher.

To be individually accountable even though they are working together, each teammember is responsible for the information and keeping involved throughout the activity. To check this, the teacher monitors, the student shares/teaches his/her information to another team, or a quiz is given.

The final step is debriefing, the closure/summary of the lesson. It is a check to see if the goal was reached and how the teams worked together, as well as time to set new goals. The teacher gives the teams positive feedback.

To finish off the lesson, each teammate gives a statement of appreciation (affirmation) to his/her partner, expressing how well they worked together (an alternative to "put-downs").

What are some of the activities that have been done as a team?

First graders have found that, if they were to draw and color a picture with only three crayons, it isn't very impressive. But, if they have a partner with three crayons then six colors can make a much nicer picture.

Fourth graders have found that locating state capitols on a map and alphabetizing them is much easier with a partner. To cross-reference for accuracy, students locate spelling words together from magazines, newspapers, textbooks, and other resource materials.

Algebra students working on individual assignments, find that they learn more by comparing and justifying their answers with a partneror and/or other teams.

> Most activities/lessons which are done individually can be adjusted and adapted into a cooperative activity.

Teams can also Team Share (with another team) their answers and information, *learn from one another,* and can support their outcome or adjust accordingly.

Some guided practice papers might **not** need to be handed in for correction, because the teacher is monitoring the students' feedback. Quizzes will indicate the level of learning from this technique.

This technique cuts down on the teacher's paperwork.

Students experience success from meeting their goals and having direct input into their learning. **They build self esteem** by being able to explain to one another a concept. They can actually see a little effort getting **direct positive feedback** (from teacher and teammates).

Friendships develop from the "bonding" by working together to accomplish a task...
Could Cooperative Team Learning be one answer to our youth at risk?

Teachers feel their workload is reduced, paper load lightened ...that students are enjoying school and performing in their classes ...that they have a positive classroom management tool.

Is it any wonder that teachers across the nation are saying... *"Cooperative Team Learning is the **best** thing that happened to the classroom since..."*
© Teresa L. Cantlon

NOTES

STRUCTURING THE CLASSROOM

Section 2

TEAM SIZE

TEAM COMPOSITION

STUDENTS NO ONE WANTS IN THEIR TEAM

HOW LONG SHOULD TEAMS BE TOGETHER?

HOW OFTEN SHOULD COOPERATIVE TEAM LEARNING BE DONE?

ROOM ARRANGEMENT

RATIONALE STATEMENT

GROUND RULES

TRUSTBUILDING-BONDING

TEACHING A SOCIAL SKILL

A COOPERATIVE LESSON

DEBRIEFING

TEACHER'S ROLE

WORKSHEETS

LESSON PLAN FORMAT

This section is designed to assist educators in **successfully** structuring their classrooms for Cooperative Team Learning.

There are "Caution" Signals to aid educators. "Caution" signals indicate that often when teams do **not** work, or are having difficulty, possibly a "caution" signal might need to be observed.

Before placing students into teams, there are important decisions which the teacher has to make:

Ideal team size, composition of teams (who will be partnered with whom), classroom arrangement, stating and demonstrating the rationale (Why work in teams?) with the students.

These are the four **main reasons** teams do **not** work well. Teacher time and thought should go into set-up for:
Structuring the Classroom Successfully for Cooperative Team Learning.

TEAM SIZE

Teams of two: for initial start up and while teams are learning to work together and developing social skills. Small teams are the **most successful**. By observing hundreds of cooperative classrooms, teams of **two** appear to be the most successful for maximum interaction, and allowing the students to "teach" one another ("95% of how we learn is when we **teach** someone else."). Teachers who use teams of two boast high success ratios.

One of the major reasons teams have difficulty is team size being **too large**, resulting in all teammembers not being actively involved throughout the lesson.
If we believe the studies that,

We Learn:
70% of what is **discussed** with others.
80% of what we **experience** personally.
95% of what we **teach** someone else...
Wm. Glasser

Smaller teams, of two students have the greatest interaction opportunity. They learn **how** to share ideas, question, and explain rationale in a safe comfortable format.

Students do not come to school equipped to work in a cooperative format. They need to be **taught the social skills** to equip them to interact, get along with others, and to make friends.

So a teacher may present an academic lesson and not have to be continually "policing" the students as they work in teams. The small **team of two** is most **ideal** for meeting this objective.

Later, if more synergy, ideas, and inter-communication is desired, and teams of two-somes show continuously the appropriate skills for working well together; teams can begin sitting in diads (foursomes) **with their partner.**

They **continue as partners,** but they can also Team Share their ideas with the other team of two at their table (Table Teams).

Having one set of materials per partner-ship is important for team involvement and materials being easy to read by each student.

PURPOSE OF CONTINUING IN PARTNERS AND TEAM SHARING IN DIADS

√ **A "buy-in" to their partner,** and won't exclude him/her.

√ **Share two sets of materials** so work is right-side-up.

√ Eliminates the **barrier** of being two desks apart or **across the table from one another.** If materials are upside down, this is a natural **break** in bonding.

Therefore, being side-by-side reinforces the the bonding between partners. Team Sharing offers the feeling of short term and occasional interacting.

When teams of two are in diads-foursomes and one student is **absent,** there is a natural team of the remaining threesome as a temporary team.

Bonding is already in place due to the nearness of their seating arrangement, and the interactions which have occurred during Team Share sessions.
Caution when seated in diads: noise level rises, more off-task behavior with partner teams interacting with the team across from them.

Teams of Three:
Teams of three-somes may have to be formed for the following reasons:

√ an **uneven class size**

√ a **chronic absentee** (might be placed in a triad to ensure an intact team)

√ a **mainstreamed,** or

√ a very **low achieving student** (might be placed in a triad to pivot off two team-members and **not** consume too much of one teammember's time).

NOTE: When a team of three must be incorporated in a classroom of pairs, **position these teams** as close as possible to the pivotal position of the instructor, (where the teacher spends most of his/her time instructing).

These are the teams (3's) which will need **guidance** in keeping every teammember involved and included **throughout** the activity. They take longer to do the task and are noisier than partner teams.

Roles usually **will not** keep all three teammembers involved throughout the activity because someone is *waiting* for his/her turn to do their part.

HINT: Keeping teams the same for all cooperative activities allows "bonding" and trustbuilding to develop.

If students sit **side-by-side** throughout a class session, *natural bonding* will continue and develop more quickly than if teams are only brought together occasionally.

The bond/trust level *breaks* every time the team is *separated* for even a short length of time.

Once teammembers are separated, it is very likely that rebonding will be necessary. *"Are we still friends?" "Can I still trust you?"* are unspoken concerns once teammembers have been apart.

 If teams are not working well together after being separated, it might mean that **trustbuilding** activities need to be reinstated. Refer to: Trustbuilding-Bonding- pgs. 13, 14, 27-29, 68

TEAM COMPOSITION

Heterogeneous Grouping
Taking into consideration:

 Often, some teams do **not** work well together because of their **team composition**. Teacher time, thought, and planning should go into the combining of students into their teams.

Some classes or groups of students are arranged homogeneously. There is still some **heterogeneity** within a homogeneous group.

Ways students might be grouped are by: **academic** level, **gender** (it is a nice discipline control tool to use girl-boy combos), **race**, **personality, bi-lingual, learning styles, social skills**, etc.

 Teams are **teacher selected:**
If students select their own teams /partners, they will choose their friends. "Like" students (students with similarities) will be teamed. Diversity strengthens teams.

 Avoid **random selection**.
When random selection is done, there is a possibility of: high students being in one team, lows in another, and discipline problems in another. Random selection is a reason why teams often do **not** work.

Ways to Group Heterogeneously

Placement by Academics and Gender

Arrange a class list of your students from high to low academically.

Place students together whose skills are **not too far apart**. If they are too far apart, they lack having things in common (vocabulary, skills, etc.) and one partner may dominate the team.

If their skills are **too close together**, academically or socially, there will **not** be enough divergence of skills to contribute to the team.

Take into consideration gender, when putting teams together: Example:

Jason	high	and	**Tara**	ave.
Jenny	high ave.	and	**Brian**	low
Terry	average	and	**Mary**	low

Girl-Boy teams are a positive class-room management tool. Often teams of any size, of the same gender, might "compete" or become rivals.

Girl-Boy combinations also allow students to share ideas, opinions and differences. Students **get to know** one another and learn what one another has to contribute from a different point of view.

Placement by Social Skills and Gender

General observation by the teacher can determine who has appropriate or inappropriate social skill behavior, as well as personality traits.

Avoid placing students together with "like" personality/behavior traits.

E.g., Teaming two shy students will not offer them a model of outgoing behavior. **Likewise,** by teaming students with behavior difficulties will only reinforce "like" (inappropriate) behavior.

Girl-boy combinations are good here, often a "nurturing" occurs. **Eg.,** shy girl with out-going boy.

Behavior/Social Skill Placement by Socio-Gram

Another option for placing students according to their social skills is by the use of a socio-gram:

A simple socio-gram might be to have each student **write their own name** in the middle of a card.

Across the top of the card they write the name of **four or five** students, (possibly of both genders) from this classroom, that they wouldn't mind... inviting to a party, (taking to the___, stranded on an island, go to the movies, etc.). **Don't ask,** *"Who you would like to work with or sit by?"* They will be disappointed when they don't get their choices!

Steve   Joan   Sunni   Rick
Teresa Cantlon
Not: Jennifer

In classrooms, usually with older students, there are those who possibly may have a direct conflict with another student. **Avoid** placing these rivals in the same team, *initially,* until they have acquired social skills to help them resolve their differences.

Instruct the students on their socio-gram card to write (if appropriate) across the bottom of their card the name of someone they believe they absolutely **cannot** sit by.

Ways to Use Socio-Gram Information

Tally by each student's name the number of times their name was recorded across the top of a card:

Jennifer I

John IIII

Ann III

Bob 0

Now organize them high to low according to number of tallies:

John   4

Ann   3

Jennifer   1

Bob   0

Students can now be placed in boy-girl combinations with another student with **higher** social skills. Place students that received **zeros** or ones with students with **three tallies or higher,** for best results in building social skills. Refer to Appendix page 164 for more details for socio-gram grouping.

Example:

John 4 - Jennifer 1
Ann 3 - Bob 0

Now you have a list of students whom your students would like to sit by. Do you place them with someone they put on their list...?

NO! These are their <u>friends</u>, and they will probably be chatting and not on task. In addition, friends usually have "like" skills and abilities.

DO NOT place anyone from their socio-gram on their team *initially,* including the person they do not want to be with.

Often teachers **omit** the suggestion of the name on the bottom of the socio-gram and place students together initially who are "enemies."

This becomes a "high risk" team. It will take a great deal of teacher time and supervision to help this team become successful.

It is better **not** to place these combinations together until much later...when they have acquired and used the social skills necessary to work successfully with someone they do not like.

NOTE: For a primary classroom, the teacher can individually **ask** a student to name four-five students they would like to play with, etc.

Another option is, using a class picture, have a child point to the faces of 4-5 students as the teacher records the feedback.

As time passes, students become adjusted to teamwork and the social expectations of working together. Many **positive** behaviors begin to emerge...

Some students actually approach their teacher and announce, *"You can take ____'s name off the bottom of my card. I think we can make things work now!"*

Others will say, *"I didn't think I would like my partner, but since we've been working together, we've become friends!"*

Students No One Wants In Their Team

Using the Socio-Gram, a student, "Jason," might not be chosen by anyone, but, Jason put down the name of students with whom he wouldn't mind working or sitting by.

Consider matching Jason with some-one who was on his list of the **opposite** gender.

Before placing the students in teams, **talk** with the student you have chosen to be with Jason. **Share** <u>honestly</u> and <u>privately</u> with the student "why" you are asking her to be Jason's partner:

> • **She exhibits many skills** which are very appropriate, takes turns, listens to others, is encouraging, etc.

> • **List these skills** to her so she can model them when in a team setting with Jason.

> • **Mention** you would like her to be Jason's partner. Jason also has some skills which can benefit a team.

 • **Give a timeline...**

You, the teacher, are asking her to be Jason's partner for <u>only</u> two weeks. If at the end of this time she feels the partnership is totally unbearable, you will allow a change of partners.

What teachers usually report is that the team with a "Jason" has <u>bonded</u> so well that there is no mention of a "break up" after two weeks.

Grouping By Learning Styles

Make a determination of students' learning styles.
(Informal Learning Preferences Inventory found in Appendix page 137).

A teacher can place students in teams by learning styles to enhance and strengthen the team's performance.
Example: Place a visual student and an auditory student together, reinforcing the weaker learning style of each teammember.

Putting two students with identical learning styles together in a team will <u>not</u> strengthen their resources.

Students with limited English/bi-lingual skills should be placed in a team with a partner who exhibits higher English speaking/reading skills to be a model for their partner.

What safer environment to practice their English speaking/reading skills but in a small team with a partner?

To cut down discrimination, do not put students of the same race in teams. Allow all students the opportunity to get to know one another, share opinions, differences and learn one another's strengths.

NOTE: When forming teams, **all** of the options suggested <u>do not</u> always have to be taken into consideration. **Choose** one option plus gender each time you make a decision to change teams and <u>vary</u> them for diversity of teaming.

How Long Should Teams Be Together?

Younger students K-2, bond quickly. Therefore, they make "fast" friends and become quite "social" very quickly.

Therefore, if teams are used frequently, (once a day) **or** if they sit side-by-side throughout the school day, they will bond quickly and **two weeks** will be enough.

Older students take longer to bond and to have a "buy-in" to their team. It will probably take a minimum of **two to three weeks** for them to experience the feeling of "teamness." They might successfully continue in their team for 2-4 weeks before teams need to change.

You will know that teams have been together **too long** when they become "best buddies" and too social.

Being together **too long** results in **ineffective** teams and exhausting the team's resources. Teams' effectiveness will go downhill very quickly if together too long. Teams begin peaking at about 3-4 weeks. Some teachers share that their teams were doing so well about 4-5 weeks ago, now they are not working well. This is a clue that they have been together <u>too long</u> and their effectiveness is declining very quickly.

Some teachers put **natural breaking points** on team longevity, *"When we reach page 92, we will change teams."*
The end of a chapter, unit, or project are all natural breaking points for team "break up."

It is important that the students have some idea as to when the "break up" will occur, so to prepare themselves to leave their "new friend."
Team Break Up: Allow partners to do a break up activity together to say *"good by."*

Break up activities could include:

- Having a team picture taken

- Draw a picture for your partner (primary)

- Write a note (letter) to your partner

- Autograph or telephone number exchanges

- "The reason you were a good partner..."
  Starter statement to finish to your partner.

- Do a *"What we have in common, Do not have in common,"* page together. (Has it changed since first becoming partners?)

- Do your team handshake, rap, chant or "whoop" for the last time.

- A last affirmation/appreciation statement

- A name adjective for your partner
  Refer to:Trustbuilding, pages 13, 44, 59

- Use your imagination

- Ask the students for suggestions

How Often Should Cooperative Team Learning Be Done?

Studies show that if teams are used a <u>minimum</u> of three times a week, academic achievement will increase. However, if teams are used this infrequently, it will <u>take longer</u> to bond and improve their social skill behavior, or to be able to work together success-fully.but, with students sitting side-by-side on a daily basis, <u>bonding occurs</u> throughout the day.

This also allows the teacher to implement the Simple Structures of cooperative learning to keep students involved. *"Think, turn to your Partner, Share, Teams Stand when..."*

When first implementing Team Learning, the teacher should start <u>slowly</u>.

We often give up on something if we do not meet with immediate success. It is important not only for the teacher but for the students to meet with success when working together.

Start with some of the Simple Structures as suggested, Partner Share, Team Stand when...,O R

"Write and then Share with your partner..."

When a teacher and the students are feeling comfortable being with a partner and doing these Simple Structures, other elements can be added.
E.g., *"Using one worksheet and pencil per Partner Team, do the questions in* Round Robin *format (taking turns)."*

If students begin saying *"Do we <u>have</u> to do this in teams?"* (after they have been enjoying team work), then "overdose" has probably occurred. Evaluate whether the time spent in teamwork needs to be cut back.

<u>**Author's note:**</u> I have heard of no cases of students "O.D.ing" on teamwork, but be aware of the warning signs.

Remember: Cooperative learning strategies will **not** be the only teaching techniques which a teacher uses throughout the class day or session. By using a variety of strategies, we will meet a greater number of students' learning styles, raise thinking skills by allowing students to share and reflect out loud and meet social skill needs.

ROOM ARRANGEMENT

It sounds simple enough, but I have walked into many classrooms, even with teams of <u>two,</u> and because of the seating arrangement of the teams, they were **not** reaching a <u>high level of success.</u>

TWO's

NOT

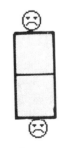

Partners sit side-by side.

Too much space between partners
Work is upside down
Noise level rises.

PARTNERS - Team Share

Until **most teams** frequently meet a <u>high level of success</u> when working together, it is probably not wise to put another team across from them in **diads** (Table Teams).

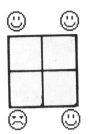

REASON:

If I haven't *bonded* closely with my partner, there are two other folks I can interact with.

Leaving **out** at least one other person.

Once partner teams have been successful for an **extended** period of time, diads are an option. Diads (Table Teams) are an option with either four desks pushed together, or two sets of partners at tables .

Keep in mind with Diads- (foursomes) Table Teams:

√ **Retain** the teams as "partner teams" and have them "Team Share" with the team across from them.

√ When using limited or shared materials, two sets (one for each team), should be available. No material should be viewed upside down.

√ **When teams stay intact** as *Partner Teams* (<u>partners</u> in a foursome), there is: m o r e interaction, sharing of ideas and classroom management control (In contrast to teams of four).

THREE's

Threesomes are difficult. Seating arrangement is tricky to keep everyone involved and included throughout an activity.

Three desks in a **pod**, by its structure, leaves one person out...

Two desks apart for one student.
Work upside down.

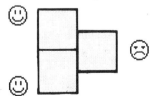

Students in a horseshoe or row, the interaction is basically with the person next to- or closest to-them.

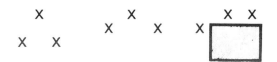

When in a tight circle there is at least one person's back to the front (teacher). If there are some teams of three in your classroom be aware of the possible difficulties.

Regardless of team size:

√ Make sure there are **no backs** to the front (teacher). When there are backs toward the teacher the bond breaks between student and teacher. Also, listening and active participation stops.

√ Put little distance between partners, (not two desks apart). Students do not feel as bonded and do not work as closely when desks.chairs are apart. Noise level also rises.

√ Partners are **seated side-by-side**, (work is right side up).

Draw a diagram of your classroom arrangement:
Make sure that **all** students can see the front of the room with little difficulty, **no backs** to the front of the room or to the teacher.
Refer to page 155 and 155a for effective classroom arrangement ideas-including chairs with arms.

RATIONALE STATEMENT

Often teachers begin putting students into teams <u>without</u> an **explanation** or **rationale** as to "why" they are being put into teams, or the expectations and benefits of working with a partner.

Students begin mumbling, *"What are we doing now?" "What's this all about?" "Dumb!"*

This is why in some classrooms team learning gets off to a shaky start. To avoid this questioning and doubt, have a <u>rationale statement</u> ready to explain to the students. Include the students in the statements. Ask them **why** they will be working in teams, the **benefits** of working with others. Share **how long** they will be working in **this** team, two to four weeks or (until they are successful, etc.).

State that they may or may <u>not</u> be with someone that is a close friend, but there are certain <u>behavior</u> <u>expectations</u> while in teams.. These will probably be the Ground Rules chosen to keep the student actively involved.

Share this statement **before** students move into their teams. Discuss and have the students **share** and demonstrate to you appropriate behavior while working in a team setting. e.g.. Quiet voices, encourage your partner (no put-downs), taking turns, etc.

This is to avoid the making of faces or name-calling to their new partners or mumbling questions like, *"Why are we doing this?"* *"You're my partner!?"*

The students need a rationale as to "why" they will be working together, e.g.,*"Why are two heads are better than one...?"* Get the students involved as to *"Why work in teams?"*
Refer to pages 20 & 21

Some teachers have discussions with the students sharing the purpose and benefits of working together.

Others give a homework assignment with the students interviewing their parents, *"Is working with others important in your work?"*

Still others give their students a "mind teaser" type of question to do by themselves, then a similar question for them to do with a partner followed by discussion.

The rationale and purpose statement should not stop with the students. It is important that **parents** and the **community** understand how cooperative team learning benefits students with lifeskills in the family, job, and community.

Letter to parents: send an introduction to cooperative learning to parents which includes; rationale, benefits, format, student's responsibility in a team, and if and how **grading** and **evaluation** will be affected by working in teams. Include if there will be less paperwork coming home and the teacher's role.

Extend an invitation to parents to view this learning structure in your classroom, so they can acquire a closer understanding of the technique and structure. Refer to page 22

Videotape a cooperative learning lesson , or activity and edit it down to 10-15 minutes. Working parents who can't take time off from their job can view the video at home.

This video will be useful during Parent-Teacher-Student-Conferences, Back to School or Open-School Nights, Staff and School Board Meetings.

 Newspaper articles in the local paper and newsletters from school. These inform parents and the community of the benefits and positive impact of cooperative team learning.

NOW IT'S TIME TO BEGIN!

You have made a decision on ideal team size and what criteria you are going to use to partner students together.

You have your classroom arrangement so partners are sitting side-by-side with no backs to the front or teacher.

Threesomes are close to your interaction area for close supervision.

You had an activity and class discussion about working in teams and its benefits. Now, the students are sitting side-by-side.

REMEMBER: the first activity before going on is for the partners to **bond** and build trust with one another.

The reason some teams do not work well together is because they do **not** know one another and feel uncomfortable with their partner. They need "bonding."

Do Short Trustbuilding - Bonding Activities

When forming new teams or when partners have been separated for more than a day.
Do one or two activities so teammates can "bond," build rapport, and trust when working with one another. These activities can be as short as two minutes or as long as it takes to complete the task (objective or activity).

Activity examples: for all levels
- **Find** commonalties, differences, likes, dislikes.
- **Share** siblings, families, etc.
- **Discuss favorites:** sports, hobbies,foods, TV programs, movies, pets, vacations, etc.
- **Do** an activity sheet together. Age appropriate crossword puzzle, Word Search, find the ___, or solve a problem together, etc.
- Any activity which requires verbal interaction.

SECONDARY- bonding activities

Do several of the above activities before doing the following:
Non academic "fun" activity
E.g., Mind puzzles, thinking games, Find the missing___. Synergy-type activities, *"If you were stranded in the desert what ten items, in order, would you choose...?"*

-Guided practice activities
Using one textbook, answer questions independently, compare answers for agreement, and discuss difference of opinion, (using review materials).

-Story problems -Partners reach agreement by discussing their answers and why.

-End of chapter/unit questions
For review, reach consensus about answers.

-Homework partners
Before submitting homework, compare answers, draw consensus, staple papers together to hand in, teacher corrects top paper.

-Partner reading of assignments.
Check each other for understanding.

ELEMENTARY-
bonding activities

-Puzzles
Pieces divided up between partners, rules may include: each partner, in turn, picking up one puzzle piece and saying, *"I think this piece goes here, do you agree?"* Objective: for students to take turns, verbally exchange ideas, and to build upon one another's resources.

-Assembly line product
Make a holiday card for nursing homes, children's hospitals, etc. **Cutter**, cuts the design; **paster**, pastes the design onto the card and they sign the product together. Use your imagination for many other assembly-line ideas!

-Team art project
Each student has limited colors of crayons, paint, paintbrush, scissors. To complete the project, they will have to share

-Partner reading
Take turns reading; ask one another questions.

-Make a structure
In teams with limited number of resources (25 index cards and 18 inches of tape, or 30 straws, etc.), try to make the highest and sturdiest free-standing structure.

-Make a small mural-
In teams with magazine pictures or cut-out words, paste the pictures/words of mutual agreement onto a sheet of paper.

-Short partner sharing sessions
To learn interests, birthdays, siblings, hobbies, sports, TV favorites, pets, etc. of teammates.

-Thinking games, mind-benders, age appropriate crossword puzzles, word search, etc.

-Color a picture together, solve a story problem, solve a riddle.

-Refer to: Trustbuilding-Bonding for additional activities, pages 27-29

The students are now feeling comfortable with one another. The teacher with the students set **Ground Rules.** Two to four observable, teachable, **behaviors** which will assist the partners in working successfully together. Behavior is synonymous with social skills.

GROUND RULES:
Start-up rules to assist teams while working together

OPTION I -
For setting the Ground Rules:
Thinking of your students, **choose** two to four short, concise behaviors (no more for start up) which will initially **guide** the students when working together...

Example:
- -Quiet voices
- -Take turns
- -Encourage your partner (no put-downs)

Remember: Specific, observable, teachable, behaviors. Do **not** choose such things as be polite, kind, courteous, cooperate, etc. These are values and are difficult to model and monitor.

Model:
- What **taking turns** looks and sounds like with your students.

- How a **quiet voice** would sound (so no one other than your partner can hear you).

- What you can say to someone to encourage them. *"Good job!"* - *You're on the right track!"*

-Include the **Signal to Stop** here. Tell the students what you expect them to do when the signal is given. E.g., *"Finish only the sentence you are saying, look at me, and put everything down ready to listen."*

Teachers can model, and then, have the students model during an activity, to show they understand and can implement the expected behavior from the Ground Rules.

Do not assume students know or have the same idea of a behavior as you. Your idea of quiet voices and the students' may differ. These behaviors must be modeled by the students to show the teacher they are in agreement on the behavior. This includes secondary students too!

13

SIGNAL TO STOP
Have an auditory signal to stop the teams when you need their attention.

Teach a back-up signal to use when the partners are interacting the verbal signal cannot be heard. **Back up signals can include:** ringing a bell, flipping the light switch, handclap, counting, etc.

E.g., (1) ringing a bell **(2)** followed by a <u>long</u> pause, (count 5-7 alligators) then say, **(3)** *"Everyone's attention here please, everything down."*

TEACH...this <u>Signal</u> to the students and what it means. *"When I say, 'Everyone's attention here please,' You are to stop talking, pencils down, eyes on me."*

Teachers need to be consistent with their Signal to Stop, and <u>teach</u> the signal to their classes.

PAUSE... After the Signal to Stop is given, a long pause should follow. The pause allows <u>all</u> teams to become quiet. It also allows students to "shift gears" mentally with the teacher. They are now ready for the next activity or directions which follow.

Often teachers begin talking <u>before</u> all the students are ready or quiet, not giving their full attention to the instructor. The **long pause** is an important classroom management technique.

<u>Signals Can Include:</u>

- Ringing a bell
- **Counting...**
  1-means finish your sentence
  2- everything down,
  3- eyes on me, everyone quiet...
- **"Ready position"**
- "Stop, look, listen"
- **Teacher claps-students repeat ✳**
- "Everyone's attention here.(long pause), Everything down." *
  *(This is very effective because it tells the students exactly what you want them to do).

> **✳Note:** Some schools have a schoolwide Signal to Stop, Usually a clap signal: Adult claps a pattern, students repeat. This is beneficial for getting everyone's attention in assemblies, the cafeteria and other common areas.

OPTION II
<u>For setting the Ground Rules:</u>
Do **NOT** assign rules and take data on students' behavior while they are working informally in teams doing a simple task. Do several observations over several days and de-cide from the data gathered what Ground Rule (behaviors) to choose.

OPTION III
<u>For setting the Ground Rules:</u>
Have the students give input into the Ground Rules after they have done a few cooperative activities together.

List <u>all</u> of their ideas and choose the basic three or four behaviors (social skills) as rules. These are the ones which will just help the teams function when first working together.

Be sure the rules are worded in short, concise <u>positive</u> language. So the students can remember and refer to these rules easily.

Being positive sets the feeling tone of the classroom. Instead of the rule No Put-downs, a rule such as Encourage Your Partner projects the same message. Remember, instinctively we covertly erase the negative and what do we have? <u>Put-downs!</u>

Again, the Ground Rules are those basic behaviors (social skills) that will be absolutely necessary *initially* to help partners function while working together.

Example for Option III
Teaching a social skill (ground rule behavior)
Teacher:
> *"I have explained to you the activity (lesson) that you are about to do. What behavior should I expect you to exhibit during the activity?"*

> *"Think about it, (long pause), share with your partner your idea(s)."* (30 seconds to 1 minute).

Use the Signal to Stop - pause.
> *"With your partner, decide on <u>one</u> behavior. When you have reached a decision, stand <u>quietly</u> with your partner."*

Pause, (teams begin to stand)
> *"One team standing, two teams up, etc....All teams standing."*

> *"When I point to your team, share the behavior. Other teams, if your team idea is mentioned, your team sits down and the team that shared the idea sits down. If your idea is still out there, remain standing until I call on you."*

Team Stand is an energizer, allows students to move, forces teams to arrive at quick consensus and keeps <u>everyone</u> involved.

Teacher writes: on the chalkboard, over head or large sheet of paper the <u>team</u> responses for appropriate behavior while working in a team.

The teacher can make a decision to choose one to three behaviors to emphasize during the lesson (activity).

E.g.,

Quiet voices
Take turns

"You have chosen very good (appropriate) behaviors for this activity. The two I will be watching/listening for as you work together today are: Quiet Voices and Taking Turns."

"I would like you to think about how you and your partner could Take Turns during this activity, as I have described it to you...(long pause). **With a quiet voice,** *share your idea with your partner."* (Allow as much as two minutes for partners to share their ideas to each other).

Teacher monitors the time needed and teams' discussions by wandering among teams and eavesdropping.

After the time allotment, the teacher calls on 3 or 4 teams (maximum to save time), to share ideas of how they are going to Take Turns. If the teams have not shared all the options the teacher desired, the teacher accepts the teams' ideas and adds on a suggestion. *"These are very good suggestions for Taking Turns. Another idea might be to..."*

Hint: Depending on the age appropriateness of your students, have the partners demonstrate by physically showing,(modeling or pantomiming) how they might take turns.

"You have shown me you know how to use Quiet Voices and Take Turns, these (as well as others) are the behaviors I will be checking while you are working in your teams during this activity."

Assign a Target Time: *"You will have ____ minutes to do this activity, or until 1:45."*

Warning Time:

Give the class a "warning time" to make them aware they are approaching the designated Target Time..."*You have 5 minutes remaining...*" Thus, giving teams time to summarize.

<u>Author's note:</u>
Options I & II are effective with younger students, K-2 or 3.

Option III is most effective with older students. Students have a "buy-in" to the Ground Rules. They had input into their formulation.

Regardless of the Option chosen for setting the Ground Rules: always <u>teach</u>, <u>model</u>, and have the students model the skills themselves for clarification of understanding, (at all grade levels).

Hint: Quiet Voices is a <u>must</u> and should automatically be a Ground Rule.
<u>Remember to teach:</u>
The auditory Signal to Stop and include the long pause which follows the Signal.

Avoid "killer phrases" which mentally allows a student to say *"No!"*
E.g., *"May I have your attention?"* *"Would you answer that?"* *"Can you find...?"*

A COOPERATIVE LESSON or ACTIVITY

Teams are ready to do **team activities.** This can be in the format of Simple Structures or a Cooperative Lesson.

If students sit side-by-side throughout a class session the teacher can implement the Simple Structures to keep **everyone** involved.
Refer to: Simple Structures, pages 33-39

EXAMPLES of COOPERATIVE ACTIVITIES:

The teacher gives the directions for an activity then asks: *"Turn to your Partner and Share the directions for this activity. When you and your partner agree on the directions, Team Stand quietly behind your chairs."*

"Good, you understand the directions for today's activity. The goal today (for your team to be successful), is to: finish the Study Sheet and to receive two points on your Team Card."

NOTE: One goal is usually enough, especially when starting Team Learning, or with younger students. For secondary students this goal is appropriate, but...If the time frame is limited so that many teams may not be able to finish, **avoid** setting the goal of "finishing the questions."

The teacher should set a goal that <u>most</u> <u>teams</u> will be able to achieve and meet with success.

Two Simple Structures were used here: <u>Partner-Share</u> and <u>Team Stand</u>. It is also a way for the teacher to check for understanding (instead of saying *"Are there any questions?"*). These two structures also keeps every student involved.

<u>**The activity**</u> is Guided Practice, a chapter review with questions to answer.
In a Round Robin (refer to Simple Structures, page 34) format, the partners are to take turns. Partner "A" **reads** the first question. Partner "B" **answers** the question (or looks up the answer). They both have to agree, and they both write down the answers on their own Study Sheet.

The next question, Partner "B" reads, and Partner "A" looks up the answer, and they both write the answer on their Study Sheets.

This **Round Robin** format of taking turns, reading, and answering continues until all the questions have answers.

To confirm and verify correctness of answers: partner teams take their answers to another partner team, and Team Share answers.

If they cannot reach agreement, consensus on an answer(s), they are to "prove" their answer with a rationale following the word "because." " *We believe it is _____ **because** _____.*"

Partner teams confirm and verify answers with three other partner teams. (This will solidify and confirm accuracy).

As the teacher monitors, s/he will observe team "X" with accurate answers, and might send Team "Y" with incorrect answers, to confirm answers with Team "X", and then confirm with two additional teams as well.

Next step is **Debriefing,** the summarization or closure of the activity.

PRIMARY COOPERATIVE ACTIVITY

Math generic:
"*I have given each Partner Team one paper that has squares with numerals inside. Taking turns with your partner, cut out these squares.*"

For kindergarten:
These numerals might be 0-10.(or 0-?, whatever numeral fits).

First or Second-grade: The numeral sheet might be 0-100 (or whatever fits, skip counting by 2's, 5's, 10's, etc.).

"*Now you have all the squares cut out, turn them upside down so you cannot see the numerals.*"

"*Now mix them up and evenly divide the squares between you and your partner.*"

"*Next, you will turn over your squares and place them in front of you, and your partner will turn over his/her squares and place them in front of him/her.*"

"*When I tell you to start you will, using the <u>blank</u> squared paper on your desk , take turns placing the numerals you and your partner cut out, in order from , ___ to ___.*"

"*If you have the '0', you will put the '0' in the first blank square. You will then ask your partner, 'Do you agree?'*"

"*If your partner agrees, the partner with the '1' will put the '1' in the next blank square, and ask your partner if they agree.*"

"*Could the same partner have several numerals to put in the blank squares <u>before</u> it is your partner's turn? ...Yes!*"

Teaching the Social Skill:
"*While you are doing this activity with your partner and **taking turns,** you or your partner might make a mistake. Is it okay to make a mistake?*"

"*Let's share some things we might say to your partner if they do make a mistake...*"

Soliciting ideas for "scripts" from the children, the teacher adds-on if necessary or needed:
    *It's okay, try again, I'll help you,
    Keep trying, don't give up,
    We all make mistakes...*

"*These are what you can say to your partner to help them feel better if they do make a mistake.*"

"*Your goal for your team to be successful is to take turns and put your numerals in correct order.*"

"*You will have ___ minutes* *to do this activity, or when the big hand is on the ___ .*"

"*Turn to your partner and share how you are going to take turns, what you are going to do with the numerals, and what you are going to ask your partner after you put a numeral in a blank?*"

The teacher monitors, observing the teams for accuracy in sequencing the numerals, and watching and listening for appropriate behavior (taking turns, encouraging their partners, etc.).

At this time the teacher can give feedback by awarding stickers, stamping team cards, awarding tallies, whatever is appropriate for teams who are meeting or have met the **goal.**

The teacher can send one team to another team to check one another for accuracy (Team Share).
They could then "discuss" with one another their technique for taking turns and putting the numerals in order.
Or s/he can check for correctness and question the children individually for techniques.
Or a combination of Team Share and teacher check is an option.

OPTIONS- This is a generic lesson; many ideas or lesson formats would fit. Ideas include:
Putting the alphabet in order, alphabetizing words. matching color words with colors, matching words with definitions, pictures with words, rhyming words etc.

 dog *frog*

When the children have completed the task or the Target Time is up, the teacher talks over the lesson, (Debriefing:summary/closure) with the class.

DEBRIEFING

Leave 3-10 minutes at the end of the activity to debrief with questions like these:

> Raise your hand if...
> Thumbs up if...
> Circle or draw a smile face if...
> Write about how...

Choose 3 or 4 or use your own from your observation of the teams as they were working:

> ...you and your partner took turns.
> ...you agreed most of the time.
> ...you worked equally on the assignment.
> ...you felt safe in making a mistake.
> ...your team met the **goal** today of...

Partner huddle and talk over...

> What went well in your team today?
> What did you like about working together?
> If you were the teacher, how would you change this lesson?
> How do your know your team used quiet voices?
> What did you learn from your teammate today?
> What did you learn from another team?
> Did you always say "because" and give a reason for your answer?
> What did you do to accomplish (or meet) the GOAL for today's activity?

If you and your partner met the *goal* of ___, give your team handshake and rap!

Include an appreciation (affirmation) statement, "Share with your partner how well you worked together today." It is important that students learn how to affirm one another in a positive format (an alternative to put-downs).

OTHER:

Debriefing can also be done in written form, in journal format, or from a questionnaire.

Debriefing should be done orally as much as possible so students can get feedback from one another and the teacher. They need to "hear" if they met their goal, what went well, and what they can work on next time.

Team Share (sharing with another team) is a component of debriefing, and can be considered part of the summary/closure of the lesson.
Refer to:Debriefing Highlights, pages 59-65

TEACHER'S ROLE:

As the teams are working together:
Observe verbal and nonverbal interaction between teammates.

Give feedback: As you, the teacher, observe appropriate behavior, give tallies on Team Cards, stamp papers, record in the grade book or on a form (with team names) on a clipboard.

Stamping Team Cards, awarding tallies, IIII bonus points, (or other formats) is giving students immediate, positive feedback. This feedback says they are meeting the goal, following the Ground Rules, or following the academic lesson appropriately.

Specific positive praising: As you monitor teams, praise behavior, work habits, etc. so the team being praised will be reinforced, but also so other teams will "over-hear" and follow the lead.
Be specific: *"Good job of taking turns."*
This **specific, positive** reinforcement, will encourage the students (teams) to continue this behavior.

OR: Take as much verbatim data as possible on appropriate and inappropriate team behavior and offer the feedback on their **appropriate behavior** (academic and/or social) during debriefing session. This compiled data will be helpful when making decisions about additional cooperative rules or social skills which need to be taught.

Save the **inappropriate** behavior for the next lesson, and teach it as a **social skill** and what the teams need to do to meet the goal for this behavior.

E.g., *"Yesterday while you were working in teams I heard some comments like these, 'Shut-up, You're stupid, That's wrong.' Today I will be listening for encouraging comments such as..."*

Have the students give suggestions as to what they might say to encourage their partner, or if their partner made a mistake, what could they say?
Refer to: Example for Option III, Teaching a Social Skill, page 14

Several appropriate "scripts" are listed from input given by the students and teacher.
*"As you are working today, I will be listening for these positive encouragements. Your **goal** as a team (to be successful), is to receive two tallies (stamps, etc) when I overhear these statements."*

Initially, these "scripts" of encouragement may sound phony and insincere or only stated when the teacher is near. It is okay to start with "phony caring," because, after additional use, it will become mechanical and routine and sincere on the students' part.

Try **not** to intervene, allow the students to work out their differences. This is one of the students' most frequent complaint, *"Our teacher won't let us solve our own problems."*

17

Evaluate:
Take 5 minutes to write down your overview of the session.
- -What went well...
- -What needs to be improved...
- -Social skills observed...
- -Social skills not observed, but needed...

Try **not** to make any changes in teams or rules until you have gathered data from several cooperative team sessions and begin to notice a pattern develop which needs correcting.

Be prepared! There may be tears, possessive behavior, resistance, displeasure and frustration (from some students and on your part too!).

Persevere: These anxieties will pass with familiarity and the students' knowledge of expectations. The *frequency* of team activities will determine the rate of success in students working compatibly.

The more frequently cooperative learning is used and if the students are sitting side-by-side continuously, throughout the class session the success rate will increase.

SUGGESTIONS:

Plan a cooperative activity with another teacher. Each teacher does the identical format with their own students. After the lesson, share together your data and evaluation, how you might set up the lesson differently, the <u>strengths</u> of the lesson and what your next activity, social skill, or goal for the students might be.

Videotape a start-up lesson for you (and a colleague) to critique. Tape another lesson several weeks later to note the social development/improvement in the teams.

Often teachers do not realize how much progress their teams have made, because they are with the students on a daily basis. **Comparing a video** of Team Learning after several weeks allows the teacher to check back on the progress and share in the accomplishment and growth of their students' team skills (social and academic).

Share this video with the students: Allow the students to see what they are doing well and what skill(s) they might want to **set a goal** toward improving.

Videotaping (edited) is also useful for Parent-Student-Teacher Conferences, Open House, as well as Staff and Board Meetings to illustrate Cooperative Team Learning.

Do A Student Attitude Survey: We have many ways of checking for academic achievement. Although we know that attitude and self esteem have an influence on learning, we very rarely measure or check student attitudes.

Included in the Appendix, pages 134-136 is a Student Survey on Attitudes about self and school for grades 4-12.

Feel free to use this survey to check and monitor your students in the classroom or schoolwide. My request is that you share the results with me.

Teresa Cantlon
PO Box 19044
Portland, OR 97219

NOTES:

NOTES

The next worksheets are designed to assist you in making decisions when structuring your classroom for Team Learning

✗ **How many** students are you going to place in each of your cooperative learning teams?

✗ **Initially**, how are you going to <u>heterogeneously</u> divide your students to make teams? (list the criteria).

✗ **Make a sketch** of your cooperative teams in their classroom arrangement, include desks (tables) and chairs.

> **Reminder:** when students are side-by-side, they "link" better, and can view materials right-side-up. Any three-somes should be close to the front of the class, **no backs** to the front or to the teacher. Keep in mind all the areas you might move to for instruction.

✗ **What** trustbuilding activities will you do **prior** to teams doing a lesson together for "bonding" to occur?

✗ **What** behaviors/socials skills will you choose (with the students) for the **Ground Rules** when first beginning team activities?

✗ Your **signal to stop is...?** Your **back up signal** when the students are interacting will be...? Followed by your verbal signal.

> **REMEMBER:**
> Specific, observable, teachable <u>behaviors</u>, **not** cooperate, be polite, be kind, respect others, etc.. These are values, **not** teachable behaviors (social skills).

Rules should be positive, **short** and **concise**, not wordy or long phrases. This makes them easier for students to remember.

✗ **Rewards/Goals:** initially, are you giving rewards, (praise, stickers, tallies, bonus points, etc.) to change behavior patterns?. If so, what must a **team** do to obtain the reward, how **immediate**? Is it an ongoing reward, or renewed activity by activity?
E.g., Bonus points: 25 = Skipped assignment for all members of the team.

✗ **How** are you going to **keep track** of points, rewards or recognition of teams? This should be <u>easy</u> and <u>convenient</u> for you to assess and monitor.

Before you put the students into teams...

✗ **What** is your **rationale** statement to the students for the following:

<u>What</u> are the **benefits**?

<u>Why</u> are they working in teams ?

<u>How long</u> will they be in this team?

<u>How</u> will they be **assessed/graded**?

<u>How often</u> will they be working in teams?

<u>What</u> are the **behavior expectations** while working in a team?
(These will probably be the Ground Rules).

<u>What</u> <u>happens</u> if they are in a team with someone they **do not** like?
Prepare students ahead of time so this feeling and questions can be avoided.
Refer to pages 21 & 22 for ideas

<u>Include students' input in the above rationale</u>: • *"Why do you think working with someone else is important?"* • *"What should your behavior be while working with a partner?"* • *"How should you react if you learn your partner is not a close friend?"*

> **REMEMBER:** You are <u>not</u> going to "break up" teams without giving them a <u>timeline</u> to "try" to be successful.

RATIONALE TO STUDENTS

Excerpt from Susan Huffmyer to her students:

"...I will assign new partners after three to five weeks. I'll make that decision by choosing people whom I think can best help each other. It's important for me to make that decision rather than allowing you to choose your friends.

I will try to pick people that will help you learn as much as possible. Again, it's important that you get a chance to meet new people. There is a possibility that you will be asked to work with someone that you do not like. You have to realize that when you get a job you won't be asked who you want to work with.

It's necessary for all of us to learn to work with people who have different personalities than those we would choose as friends. But you may find out that a person that you thought you didn't like is really very nice.

If you have some serious problem with compatibility, you will need to be with your partner at least one week before checking with me and we will try to resolve it.

...The last thing I want to tell you about is your grade. You will be asked to work with other students to discuss, to review, and possibly to do a project. But your grade, that appears on your report card, will be based on what you do independently on quizzes and tests. Points you earn as a group will be counted as extra credit. So the work you do while you are in groups can only help your grade."

Excerpt from Julie Nisley to her students:

"You are going to have the opportunity to enjoy school with someone in the class that you probably don't know very well. Your partner is your helper. With one exception, feel free to go to him/her whenever you need assistance.

What would be the exception? " (tests)

RATIONALE STATEMENT

Thinking of the benefits of cooperative learning, develop a rationale statement which you will address to <u>parents</u> explaining <u>why</u> their student will be working in small cooperative teams.

KEEP IN MIND-
√ The <u>role of the teacher</u>, grading procedure, will the paperwork coming home decrease, the <u>benefits</u> for the student (when you reflect outloud is how you learn best, students can meet and make new friends, give reason/rationale for their answers, thus raising thinking and processing skills). Include <u>future</u> benefits, (to assist in working and getting along with others, sharing ideas and disagreing with opinions without criticizing others, etc.). Cooperative learning develops and puts into application the much needed <u>social skills</u> which apply to not only to school, but life.

√ This is <u>not</u> the only format for learning, but will be <u>one</u> of the structures used in your classroom.

√ Cooperative learning is research based. It is <u>not</u> a new idea, but it has not been used for the past four or five decades.

√ End with an **open invitation** welcoming them to visit the classroom to see this highly effective teaching-learning strategy in action!

LESSON PLAN

Using the Lesson Plan format, as a guide, (next page and Appendix, page 138, in addition to the Lesson Plans provided on pages 95-122) **complete a lesson in a subject area of your choice to include the following:**

√ **Debriefing**
Specific debriefing questions.

√ **Roles, if assigned**
The specific responsibility of the role. How the roles will be <u>introduced</u> to teams. They can be a part of the directions.
E.g., *"Blue dot partner will do ___. Red dot partner will have the job of ___."*

If the roles have a "script," how will this be introduced to the teams?
E.g., *"Today while working with you partner it is important to encourage one another. If you say 'good job' to your partner or other encouragers, put a tally mark on the top of your paper."*

√ **Rules - Social Skills**
What are the cooperative team ground rules and signal to stop? How are they integrated into the lesson? If they have already been taught, are they just reviewed? Or is a new rule-social skill going to be introduced?
E.g., *"I have noticed as you were working with your partner many teams were not taking turns equally. I want you to think about ways you and your partner can take turns evenly."* Pause
"When I say 'go' discuss with your partner ideas on how to take turns equally and how you can monitor taking turns. For example, you might use a different color ink or lead. Go."

√ **Goal**
What is the team goal, criteria for success? Is it attainable by nearly<u> all</u> teams? What is the <u>specific</u> statement to the teams? What do they have to do to meet with success?
E.g., *"If your team finishes the activity in the allotted time, you are successful."* **OR** *"If your team accomplishes 5 out of 8, your team is successful."* **OR** *"If your team gives one another five encouragements, during this activity your team is successful."*

If the team is successful the "reward" can be as <u>simple</u> as, *"It your team met the goal of completing at least 5...Stand and give your partner a high-five and say, 'we did it!' "*

LESSON PLAN FORMAT for COOPERATIVE LEARNING
To use as a **guideline**, write on your own paper for more space.

TEAM SIZE:

TIME LIMIT for entire lesson:
TARGET TIME for Student work:

TEAM COMPOSITION: heterogeneous by...
•

ACTIVITY: lesson to be done...
•

GROUND RULE or SOCIAL SKILL (emphasized during this lesson)
•
•

The way this social skill will be emphasized is by: E.g., Going over scripts, modeling, reviewing, etc.
•

-- Signal to stop is ... •
--Back-Up signal is...•
(when students are interacting and a voice is not affective)

MATERIALS: shared or limited ?
•
•

ROLES: If necessary and appropriate. If assigned, what is the responsibility of the role?.
•

GOAL+ reward = feedback:
What the TEAM must do to be successful, and how they know they have accomplished the goal-reward/feedback system.
•
•

INDIVIDUAL ACCOUNTABILITY:
How will the teacher monitor students' knowledge: random checking, post-test, etc.

•

•

DEBRIEFING: summary and closure of the lesson
List specific questions which reflect back on the lesson. To be asked after the cooperative activity. What formats will be incorporated? E.g., Thumbs Up, Partner Share, Team Stand, Team Share, Interview, etc.
•
•
•

The teacher debriefs last with specific feedback from observation data, Student Debriefing Forms, or from the Team Cards on the students' desks.

Note: remember to encourage students to include an appreciation statement (affirm one another).
E.g., *"Share with you partner ways he/she helped you today."*
Refer to: pages 95-122 for lesson plan formatting ideas

NOTES

TRUSTBUILDING - BONDING

Section 3

NOTES

Trustbuilding should be the <u>first</u> <u>activity</u> of a Cooperative Learning lesson when <u>new</u> <u>teams</u> <u>are</u> <u>formed</u>.

Although students might already know one another, this does not mean they have worked in a small team together. *"Can I make a mistake with you, or will you put me down?"*

When teams don't work well together, it is often the result of trust or bonding <u>not</u> being established. *"I really don't know you, can I trust you?" "Will you accept me?"*

If Cooperative Learning is done infrequently (2-3 times a week), or if teammembers do not sit together (side-by-side) through-out the day, a trustbuilding-bonding activity can be used as a transition into the cooperative lesson. <u>It</u> <u>helps</u> <u>rebond</u> <u>the</u> <u>teammembers</u>.

Unspoken concerns might be:
"We have been apart; can I still make a mistake with you; are we still friends.?"

> Trustbuilding activities can take 2-5 minutes, or they can comprise an entire lesson or activity.

If a teammember is absent and a student has to be placed with a new partner, be sure to give the new partners a few minutes to bond:

<u>E.g.,</u> *"While I am passing out papers, you and your new partner discuss your favorite..."* (T.V program, music, food, sport, etc.)

This allows the new partners to become acquainted so they can go on with the cooperative task without wondering *"Who is this person; do we have anything in common?"*

How will you know if the partners are not bonded?
If one or more teammembers in the team fold their arms, turn their backs to their teammate, or refuse to work, it is highly probable that more bonding - trustbuilding needs to take place for that team.

What does a teacher do if one or more teams have not bonded?
Give these teams more trustbuilding opportunities with activities (goals) to accomplish together. Teammembers need to know they have something in common, and are working together toward a common goal. To be <u>successful</u> they need to work together <u>comfortably</u> <u>and</u> <u>compatibly.</u>

INTERVIEW:
Students interview one another in partners, then introduce their partner to another team, and tell something they learned about their partner.

COMMONALTIES:
In teams, students try to find three (or any number) things they have in common. On a piece of paper, teammembers write their names on either side and in the middle "What we have in common..."

What WE have in common		
Jason		Amy
football	pizza, dancing, red,	tennis
	2 brothers, math	

Unusual, unique, interesting, are words which could be added to the directions to enhance discussion (refer to Appendix for Venn diagram example).

Option: Have the teams, on one piece of paper, write Dislike - Like across the top of the paper.
Along the side, going down, have topics such as: Food, Sport, Animal, Music, etc.

As a team the partners must come to agreement on one item for food that they both like and one food item they both dislike.

Partners:_____ and _____

                LIKE   DISLIKE

FOOD
T.V.
MOVIE
MUSIC
ANIMAL
DESSERT
Other:

NAME THAT TEAM:
Each team comes up with, any or all of the following: team name, handshake or greeting , and a chant or "rap"
They can do these at appropriate times with their teammembers, e.g., when they have met their goal.

For young children: They may decide together on a favorite animal (real or imaginary),draw a picture of it together on a team card (4X6 card), and make up a "noise or sound" their animal makes.

MOBILES - CRESTS - LOGOS - BANNERS:
Partners can design a TEAM mobile to hang over their team table (desks) which identifies them as a team.

A team creset (coat of arms) can be designed to show a "we" team. The teacher, when awarding stickers, stamps, tallies, etc. might affix them to the team crest (shield).

Team logos are fun for the team to develop together. They "design" a picture, words, etc. which is their identification or label. These may be a part of the Team Card or used on a banner or sign on their team desk(s) for identification.

For Secondary: Tape a manila envelope on the side of the team desks. Each class session, teams can pull out their Team Cards, sign, etc.

PANTOMIME:
Step I: Individuals will pantomime to each other an activity, sport, hobby, etc. that they enjoy.

Step II: The team will come up with a unified activity that they might enjoy or have in common and will pantomime this activity for another team to guess.
E.g., They both might play tennis, so they act-out this sport.

ROUND ROBIN:
In "round robin" format students will solve a crossword puzzle, mind bender, word search, scrambled words, story problems, work sheet, etc. by working together and passing the paper/pencil to their partner with each turn.

MIND MURALS:
Make a team collage from magazine pictures or words. These must be chosen by mutual team agreement. (This can be done to a theme or subject)

NAME ADJECTIVES:

Each teammember prints his/her first name vertically on a piece of paper or a 3X5 card, and exchanges the paper with another teammember.

Teammembers write a positive adjective or phrase about their teammate using each letter.

This can also be used as a "break-up" activity, when teams are going to be changed.

J	jokes a lot
O	often smiles and jokes
H	happy, fun to be around
N	never gives put-downs

REBUS PICTURE:

Individually, students draw pictures, adding letters, symbols, numerals, etc. to illustrate to their partner:
Use their name, favorite sport, food, hobby, etc. (choose one theme at a time for them to illustrate). Their partner tries to guess the Rebus Picture; they take turns sharing.

To take the Rebus Picture one step farther, partners could develop a team Rebus Picture, which they could Team Share with another team. E.g.,

CODES-CODING:

Using Morse Code, the partners would write a note, assignment or answer to a question to one another or to another designated team.

Partners could make up their own codes using the alphabet in mixed order, or new signs/symbols designed by the teams.

STARTER STATEMENTS:

Sentence Starters are fun for students of all ages to find out more about one another. In an "Interview" format, students can ask one another some predesignated questions which can be on cards or written on the backboard or overhead from suggested Sentence Starters...

My favorite sport is...

My three favorite foods are...

The food I do NOT like is...

During vacation I like to...

I wish...

I find it easy to...

I find it hard to...

One thing good about school is...

I am happy when...

I felt sad when...

Something I do well is...

Something I would like to learn to do is...

My favorite holiday is... because...

My favorite music is...

The thing that worries me most is...

When I think about the future I...

Someone I really admire is... because..

If I had a free day I would...

Animals that I like are... because...

With my friends I...

A movie I really enjoyed was... because...

My favorite book is ... because...

In my family we like to...

A hobby I enjoy is...

NOTES

Section 4

Includes:

Skill Cards

Observer

NOTES

COOPERATIVE LEARNING:

Does NOT have to be an elaborate lesson with all the elements included (social skills, debriefing, individual accountability, etc.).

Studies show that academic achievement can increase with frequent use of some of the "Simple Structures."

The "Simple Structures" can be used throughout a teacher's directed lesson, *("Huddle with your partner and share your ideas")* during review, or *("In your team, brainstorm all the possibilities")* in a more structured format.

The following pages contain ideas of "Simple Structure" activities which can be used or adapted for use throughout the teaching day.

> "Simple Structures" can be used interchangeably during a cooperative or teacher-directed lesson to keep *everyone* involved.

Most academic lessons can be adapted into a cooperative activity with little effort once a teacher becomes comfortable using the various "Simple Structures."

Author's note:
Simple structures may also be used effectively to check for understanding, as opposed to: *"Are there any questions?"*
E.g. *"Think about the instructions,* (long pause) *turn to your partner, Partner Share the instructions; when you agree, Team Stand."*

This is a quick way to check for understanding, as well as energizing the team by allowing them to stand.

The teacher can now <u>randomly</u> ask individuals to orally share their understanding of the instructions. Another option is to have the entire class orally respond in choral fashion to posed questions thereby eliminating the need for reexplanation or reteaching, and the wasting of valuable learning time.

Also, by having students explain to one another in their own vocabulary raises retention and increases higher level thinking skills. The "Teach / Explain" technique gives a new dimension to instructions when they can be explained in "kid-talk."

To set up the Simple Structures the teacher "script" is important to structure the outcome of the activity. Within the "script" a social skill can be included. E.g., *"The partner on the right will give assistance and encourage your partner by saying 'Good job."*

> Refer to page 159- for examples of Teacher "scripts" for the Simple Structures.

ROUND-ROBIN

Using one pencil/pen, one paper: One partner writes an answer/idea, then passes back the paper to his/her partner. This continues until the task is completed or time is called by the teacher.

Example (another option)
With students in teams. Give each student a worksheet of problems/questions.

Each student works on the first problem (question, etc.), then passes his/her paper to the person on his/her left, and continues to work on the second problem (question); the papers are switched again. This continues until the entire paper is completed.

The teammembers put their names on the papers, the papers are stapled together, and the teacher corrects the top paper!

Students can tutor a teammate who needs help, but the student must learn the material because the teacher could call on any teammember to share the process of how they arrived at this answer. Or a quiz, taken individually, could be given with teammember's scores averaged together for bonus points, tallies, etc.

A nice touch to Round-Robin is to give each student a different color ink/pencil so that it becomes clear who has done which problems, sentences, etc. on the worksheet.

Round-Robin may be used for "brainstorming" ideas, with each person writing down an idea or a team suggestion, and passing paper/pencil to next teammember.

> **Round Robin** is designed to keep team-members equally involved throughout the activity. It teaches the skill of "taking turns."

INTERVIEW

Interview is designed to introduce teammates to each other in some depth, as well as giving the teacher another tool to use for teaching paraphrasing. Implement this technique in the curriculum areas for students to draw information from one another or for review.

In teams of two, teammember A interviews teammember B, gathering background information which will be used to introduce each person to another set of teammembers or to the class. This is repeated with B interviewing A to share learned information to another team or to the class.

Interview can be adapted to curriculum areas, and teammates "interview" one another to gain further knowledge background from one another in a subject matter.

E.g., Solve a story problem and share with teammate step-by-step the process used for arriving at an answer: teammate (who is listening) paraphrases back the process and shares his/her process for a solution.

E.g., Have the students share techniques for studying or accomplishing homework assignments; the next day have the students describe to teammates which techniques worked best, and strategies they might try for the next assignment.

> **Interview:** Develops listening and interpreting skills, checking for understanding, higher level thinking, communication skills, and if no note-taking is emphasized, this is a lead-in skill for teaching the skill of paraphrasing.

Paraphrasing

The Interview technique can be used as a "lead-in" to teach the skill of paraphrasing.

Using the "interview" technique substituting study questions or other learned information, it will be the "interviewer's" responsibility to paraphrase, *without notes*, the "interviewee's" feedback or answers.

> **Paraphrasing** is an interpretation of the "meaning" of what was said by the interviewee, what the interviewer "believes" the interviewee "means."

PARTNER SHARE

When the teacher asks a question or is requesting a response...the teacher asks the students to *"Think over"*...(long pause) and requests *"Turn to your partner and talk it over."*

OR the term, *"Huddle with your partner(s) and talk it over."*

> **Partner Share** will allow students to "hear" others' input, confirm their own ideas, and solidify concepts as well as keeping everyone actively involved and raising higher level thinking and retention skills, by **explaining** out loud how they came up with their answer.

Refer to page 159- for "Scripts" for Simple Structures

LETTERED/NUMBERED/ COLORED HEADS or Red dot-Blue dot

Students assign themselves a letter, A or B, within their teams; the teacher asks a question. After huddling, the teacher randomly points to a team and calls out a letter. The teammember whose letter is called *responds* to the question.

Variation: To check for overall <u>understanding,</u> the teacher can ask a question, h a v e teammembers huddle, call out a letter, have all the "A's" raise their hand, pencils up or *"thumbs up"* if they have at least one answer to contribute.

If any "A"does not have an answer, those teams <u>rehuddle</u> and share information.

The teacher <u>can</u> <u>call</u> on "A's" again, or call out a <u>new</u> <u>letter</u> and repeat the procedure until all the lettered heads respond in the affirmative when their letter is called.

> Lettered heads develops listening skills, paraphrasing from others' ideas, as well as keeping everyone actively involved and participating.

Other ideas include using numbers or colors instead of letters. Self adhesive colored dots affixed to the desktops are helpful.
Respond to the student <u>by</u> <u>his/her</u> <u>name</u> after they have responded to personalize the format. <u>Or</u> when pointing to a team and calling out a letter, have the student first respond by saying his/her own name, thus helping the teacher and classmates learn everyone's name.

HINT: If students have difficulty remembering their assigned letters, numbers or colors, they may be <u>recorded</u> in front of them or placed on cards with which to refer to save time. Students are often "searching" to remember their letter/number instead of reflecting on the question asked.

> **Red-dot/Blue-dot** (Lettered Heads) allows a teacher to check for understanding and to raise the number of students involved in the activity. It develops listening and thinking skills, a n d assists in learning names, especially helpful for secondary teachers.

THINK-WRITE-PARTNER SHARE
After presenting a question, the teacher instructs the students to *"think"*...(long pause)

"write your idea(s)"...(long pause) *"share this with your partner."*

Variation: *"With your partner, decide on one idea and..."* (thumbs up or Team Stand) *"when you agree."*

> **Think-Write-Share** keeps all students involved, raises comprehension, thinking and retention skills, and is a good way to check for students' understanding.

ALL TEAMS STANDING
The teacher instructs the teams to *"Huddle"* or *"Share with your partner"* and reach agreement or consensus on a concept, <u>or</u> come up with several options and <u>choose</u> <u>one</u> as a team.
When the team has decided on <u>one</u> option, both partners stand.

Each team shares orally their idea/answer and they then sit down. If other teams <u>hear</u> their option mentioned before their turn arrives, they sit also.

NOTE: <u>Limited</u> <u>correct</u> <u>answers</u> are usually best, or every team may have a different answer. If classes are large, the answering session could be lengthy.

Guard against, *"I'll give you 5 minutes to come up with an answer, Team Stand when your team has an answer."* Some teams could be standing 4 minutes while others are working!

Instructions such as, *"Stand quietly behind your chair (beside your desk),"* will assist in the management of this structure.

> **All Teams Standing:** Keeps all teams (students) involved, develops listening skills, forces students to reach quick agreement or consensus, and is an energizer*

*Students need to stand frequently to keep up their momentum and attention span. Have you ever wondered why you might feel more tired after a day of inservice and sitting, than after a day of work, where you are moving about?

TEAMS SHARE
Teammembers within a team: <u>Share</u> information, ideas, or come up with a solution or end product. Teams then "partner" up with another team to <u>share</u> the information, answers, end product, etc.
Refer to page 159- for "scripts " for Simple Structures.

Teams Share Is a way for teams to check for accuracy, compare information from another point of view, and allows for individual accountability. They have to discuss or teach orally their information, and *"pridefully"* share their end products. It is also an energizer.

Initially the teacher should designate teams who will Team Share. Often, there is chaos when the students randomly go to other teams.

The teacher is monitoring, facilitating, and "eavesdropping" throughout the process.

Debrief: Team Share is also a "debriefing" technique as teams share what they learned from another team, *adding value* to another team's ideas.

BRAINSTORMING in teams
The 4 S's (as adapted from S. Kagan)

Have **each** teammember fold a piece of paper into eights, crease and tear on the folds. Combine these into one pile of note paper.

Given a topic or theme, teams are to have one member write one idea per piece of paper, using one pencil/pen per team and a time limit.

Using the guidelines of the 4 S's (below), teams develop as many ideas as possible. Depending on the topic, they can now categorize them physically by arranging the pieces of paper which lists the idea.

Taking the concept one step further, teams can categorize into probable or improbable, workable or unworkable, realistic or unrealistic, etc. Another reason for one idea per paper besides being able to easily categorize, is to be able to physically discard unusable ideas.

Brainstorming - 4 S's
√ Tell the teams to work fast (speed) under time constraint, coming up with as many ideas as possible writing ONE idea per piece of paper.

√ There is no evaluation of ideas (suspend judgment).

√ Encourage inclusion of all ideas (silly ideas included), all ideas help.

√ Build onto the ideas of others, *"add value"* to a suggestion or opinion (synergy).

Brainstorming techniques keep all team-members involved, allows for differences of opinions to be exercised safely, teaches how to accept an idea and "add on" (value) to the idea as opposed to total discarding of an idea, develops listening skills, working within a time frame, and categorizing.

FOLDED CORNERS -Linda Timmel
On a notepad size piece of paper, (3X3, etc) have each member of the team write his/her first and last name across one corner of the paper (if there is a team name, write it across the middle of the paper).

Have the student fold a corner of the paper over his/her name to hide the name, put these into a basket or box for easy drawing/selection.

When you want a "volunteer" answer and not only from the student with their hands raised, allow the teams a few seconds to share their ideas with their partner, draw one of the Folded Corner papers, lift one corner, and call on this student by first and last name to respond. Or, call out the team name, and have one volunteer from the team respond.

Since the teams have "shared ideas," it should be very safe to call on anyone; but if after sharing with their partner, a student still cannot respond when called upon, the teacher may:

Ask them to "rehuddle" and share an idea/ answer with their partner.
Or have another Team Share an idea/ answer.
Or move on and draw a new Folded Corners paper.

NOTE:
• Primary teachers may have to write first and last names for their students initially.

• Folded Corners can also be used when students are asked to choose another student or a volunteer. The student randomly draws a Folded Corner paper from the box and calls out a name, instead of naming best friends or students of the same gender.
Refer to: page 152 for pattern

Folded Corners assists in choosing volunteers randomly, helps teacher and students learn classmembers by first and last names, develops listening skills, keeps many involved for a good portion of the activity, and adds variety to the question/answer technique.

JIGSAW Basic -Aronson
Students are in teams. Each teammember is given or selects a topic or portion of the subject-matter to be studied.

Base team I	Base team II
A B	A B

They study specified material individually and develop ways to teach their teammate(s) this information.

Teams reorganize to form "expert" teams.

These are comprised of new teammates that have been learning (studying) the same topic. (A quick trustbuilding-bonding activity may be necessary so they feel comfortable sharing with a new teammember).

Expert team	Expert team
A A A	B B B

Students in "expert" teams share their ideas on how they might teach their topic when they return to their BASE team (original team).

After sharing ideas and strategies, students return to their BASE teams.

Teammembers take turns teaching their topics to each other (original team).

Base team I	Base team II
A B	A B

The teacher may give a quiz or assignment to test students' knowledge of subject matter learned as a team effort.

The teacher debriefs with the teams to learn how they worked while in their teams and what they might do differently next time.

VARIATIONS TO JIGSAW

JIGSAW II: everyone reads or has a summary of all the material, so that each teammember has an overview or background of what other team-members are sharing or teaching.

PARTNER JIGSAW: Partners learn information, share ideas with another set of partners with the same information (expert teams), then teach their topic or information to a **new** set of partners.

Develop your own technique or creative twist to Jigsaw. Jigsaw is an effective technique when there is a lot of information to cover, and learning only the essence or main idea is necessary.

NOTE: Jigsaw may not meet the needs of every grade level or subject matter, and may not be appropriate for primary students except in a simplified format.

PARTICIPATION CHIPS
Using colored chips (squares) of paper, paper clips, bottle caps, or anything movable:
Give each teammember an allotted number of chips.

Discuss with the students what participation means while doing team work.

Each time they participate (or talk) in their team, they "place" one of their Chips in the middle of their team table.

When a teammember is out of Chips they cannot participate (or talk) again until all the Chips from other teammembers are in the middle and the Chips are redistributed.

VARIATION:
Place Chips in the middle of each team table (desks), and each time a teammember participates (or talks), the participant takes out a Chip and places it in front of him/her.

During debriefing (summarizing/closing the lesson), ask each student to count his/her Chips, compare the numbers with their partner(s), and come to a conclusion about their participation.

Ask teams to decide how their Participation Chips could become more evenly distributed among teammembers. These answers could be shared with another team to help add ideas for participation to each team.

Do this activity at least once involving the entire class, so the students know this is an option they have available to them while working with others. and one or two participants begin dominating the team.

Participation Chips might only be necessary with an occasional team who is having difficulty "taking turns."

Participation Chips visually shows the participation of teammembers within a team. It allows teams to make goals/decisions about how they might work differently, or what they will continue doing to encourage equal participation within their team.

COLORED CARDS

Students or the teacher prepare cards (in flashcard fashion) with a question on one side, and same question with answer on the opposite side of the card.

One student has a set of cards in one color (white), and his/her partner has a set of cards in another color (blue).

Option: Prior to doing the activity, the students, individually, on their own, take a pretest on the information given on the cards.

The partners add their raw scores together and these are recorded.

The partners will now try to raise their "pretest-Base Team Score ."

Partners trade the colored cards they had originally so they have each other's cards.

They now take turns reading the question on the card, and the partner responds.

If the response is correct, the partner responding earns back, and is given, his/her card plus an encouragement. e.g.,"Good answer!"

Now, the second partner asks the first partner a question, and they continue until all the cards have been "earned" back by the cards' owner.

If an incorrect response is given, the partner asking the question offers the correct answer and a possible idea of how to remember the answer. The missed card goes to the bottom of the pile until it is "earned" back with a correct response.

Prior to doing colored cards, the teacher should review with the class "scripts" they might say to their partner if they make a mistake, or to encourage their partner:

E.g., That's okay try again,"... "You're getting better,..." "I"ll help you with this one,..." "Nice try, but the answer is..."

These (plus others) are the scripts the teacher will be monitoring while partners are "quizzing."

When the positive scripts are overheard, the teacher can award tallies, stamp a team card, give positive feedback, or make notations to give recognition during the debriefing session, after the activity.

Later, the teacher can give a post-test to the students to check for improvement in acquiring the learned information from the "flashcard" format.

Teams who have improved their scores can be awarded bonus points, tallies, stamps on their team cards, give their partner their secret handshake, or other appropriate recognition for meeting their goal of improving their score.

> Colored Cards can be used in most subject areas to review information: spelling, vocabulary, definitions, math concepts, review questions for a test, etc.

Hints:
Avoid putting numerals or letters beside multiple choice questions on the cards. Students will memorize the numerals or letters, as opposed to learning the information.

Students could make up questions, the teacher could compile the questions and use these in the Colored Card format for review and quiz on these questions.

Questions can be in True/False, Multiple Choice, Direct Answer, or any format in which there is a correct or limited answer(s).

Use a thickness of paper which allows the answers not to be seen through the card.

If the questions are not printed on both sides, partners should sit side-by-side and be able to see the written information together. The card may then be turned over to reveal the answer.

Use a limited amount of questions in each setting so the students can reach "mastery" in a short period of time:

E.g. In one eight minute setting of Color Cards format, partner teams can "master" about eight questions. The next day give a new set of eight questions, and the third day use the original sixteen (combined both days) questions for review and so on.

Note: If colored paper is not available, with colored pens, color code the cards in one corner of each set. E.g., One set has red √'s in right hand corner, the other set of cards has blue √'s.

> An example of commercial version of questions in reading and math which can be used in a Colored Card format may be found in the Appendix, pp 156 & 157.

SKILL CARDS-Encourager
To Reinforce the Social Skill of Encouragement

The student partners have a stack of small Encourager Cards in front of them.
Refer to: pp. 150 & 151 for pattern ideas

The partners work on a review assignment. While the partners are working together, IF they give their partner an encouragement, *"Good job, Rod!" "I like the way...,"* etc., the partner that **gives** the encouragement, hands their partner an **Encouragement Card** to indicate (kinesthetically) to their partner they have been given feedback.

OPTIONS:
When the academic/lesson is completed, partners count the number of Encouragement Cards they received.

Partners Share with one another two or more Encouragements they remember.

They can Team Share with another team how they earned their cards, what they said to get a card from their partner.

> Partner-and Team-Sharing of the Encouragement Card allows a reinforcement of positive encouragement and hearing a variety of "scripts."

A twist: Instead of Encouragement Cards, there could be cards for any social skill which needs reinforcement:

Taking Turns (SHARER)

Listening (LISTENER)

Participating (PARTICIPATOR)

Asking for Ideas or Opinions

(QUESTIONER)

Using Proper Names (NAMER)

Pulling Ideas Together (SUMMARIZER)

Agreeing with Another's Idea (AGREER)

Adding an Idea to Another's Thought or

Idea (VALUE ADDER)
Refer to: Appendix -Observer's Reference Form, page 141

Stay with one skill for a length of time to ensure the skill is mastered by a majority of the teams before moving on to a new skill.

OBSERVER Using skill cards

> A student(s) who does not exhibit a necessary social skill or does not work well with his/her partner could be an observer using these Skill Cards.

This student sits and observes an "exemplary" team for a length of time. (5-15 minutes).

Beforehand, the teacher shares with the "observer" which skill to watch/listen for.

Examples:
"I have a special job for you today. You will be an observer, watching Bill and Jeri as they work together.

As they are working together today, I want you to put a "participator" card in front of the partner that is participating.

Now let's talk about what "participation " means to you..."

Listen to the observer's ideas. Share your ideas. The Observer might ask the partners in the team being observed their idea(s) on *participation.*

As the team(s) begin to work, the Observer watches/listens for participation between the partners in the "exemplary" team being observed.

The Observer will give the Partner Team feedback on what they did to receive the "Participator" Skill Card(s).

This will reinforce the behavior which the observer needs to work successfully with his/her partner.

Note: Instead of skill cards, an observer could make tallies on a card beneath the participant's names:

Participator	
Jeri	Bill
II	IIII

After a time span has elapsed and the "Observer" has had other opportunities to observe and practice these skills, choose a "New Observer."

The new Observer will be watching the team with the EX-Observer, awarding Skill Cards for the appropriate behavior observed.

The "Ex-Observer" is now aware of and will model the appropriate skills for the "new Observer" to "earn" a card for him/herself or for the team!

CORNERS

> This activity can be used as an energizer, adds to class bonding, allows checking with someone other than own partner, gain new ideas. Incorporates the social skills of: coming to agreement (consensus), accepting another's opinion, as well as the skill of giving reason and rationale.

Various ways to do Corners:
When student finishes his/her assignment he/she stands and waits for the next person to stand. This person becomes their "checking partner." They partner up, go to a corner (or nearby wall) and compare information answers. If they agree, they mark their assignment accordingly. If they do not agree they must give a reason and be able to support their answer. They find a new partner, go to a new "corner" and go through their answers again. After three rotations student and teacher are assured the answers are correct.

Partner teams work on an assignment and when finished stand and wait for the next team to stand, go to a space and compare answers. The teacher should set up the rule: everyone in the team must share ___ times when you are Team Sharing in Corners. (Thereby one partner won't dominate the sharing if the rules are both partners must participate and contribute).

Corners may be used any time the teacher wants students to have new/temporary partners, to get new ideas, suggestions or sharing of opinions.
E.g., *"Go to the corner with the picture which you think best illustrates your impression of the story you just read. Share with another person in the corner why you think this picture describes the story. Take turns sharing."*

"If you had trouble with problem number 17, go to Corner ___ where Rick, Sue and Sam will assist you. If you had problem with number 29, go to Corner ___ where Ann, Rick, and Mary will assist, etc. . Remember, you will be asked to explain the problem before you leave the corner."

LINE UP

> Kinesthetic/tactile way for students to experience learning, format for sequencing, good for review and is an energizer.

Various formats:
Line Up can be used with a whole class line or with smaller lines of students.
E.g., Five in a line with several lines or three to a line, etc. throughout the classroom. No students are sitting and watching, everyone is participating.

Students are individually given information and they are to line up sequentially according to their part.
E.g., each student could have the name of a time/date in history and they are to put themselves into the line according to when they occur. (Several lines of students could be around the classroom with similar or the same information).

Line Up according to: alphabetizing, when events occur in a story, matching a date with an event, graphing, math answers according to their sequential values, states with their capitols (alphabetized), vocabulary words and their definitions, for young children they could line up by months of their birthdays, color of hair, height, size of foot etc.

BAG IT!

> Format for review, energizer, checking for understanding. Includes the social skills of sharing opinions and ideas, taking turning, coming to agreement.

Each team is given a small sealed bag with items in it which can be used for reviewing a skill. These bags can be sitting on the team desk for an entire class session before they are opened... thus adding to the suspense of Bag It!

When the signal is given the partners may open their bag and remove all the materials.

One partner at a time randomly picks up an item shares with his/her partner what he/she thinks the item represents or the answer. He/she then turns to the partner and asks, *"What do you think?"* If they agree that the item belongs in the bag it is returned to the bag, if they disagree or do not think the item belongs in the bag, it is left out.

Examples of review items for the bag:

Numbers that cannot be evenly divided, fractions that are reduced to lowest terms, words with correct definitions, dates in history with correct events, formulas which are correct, animals that are reptiles, authors /composers of the twentieth century, explorers from England, food groups, questions that are true, events that occurred, classifying, etc.

Any **review items** which can be categorized, labeled or be true/false can fall into Bag It!

Students of all ages enjoy Bag It! (secondary also) because it is a fun format for review. After the partners agree which go into the bag and which ones are left out they can go to another team and Team Share their answers by stating, *"We think this goes into the bag because..."* giving reason and rationale to convince the other team and compare answers.

Box It!

> Format for review, energizer, checking for understanding. Includes the socials skills of taking turns, sharing ideas, giving reason/rationale by saying "because," and graciously disagreeing with opinions/answers.

Materials:
• One cube/box (3"x3" or larger) • Post It sheets or squares of paper which fit the sides of the box • Writing instrument • Topics, statements, questions, or problems for each team to respond.

Each partner team looks at their statement. Taking turns they think of questions or clues which fit the statement. Each partner writes one question/clue on each slip of paper or Post It and affixes it to one side of the cube. There is a possibility of six questions/clues. Give the teams a timeline for the writing of questions. Some teams might write three clues, others may have six. This is a way to keep all teams busy by calling "time" before too many teams become "off task."

Now the partner team goes to another team and trade boxes/cubes. The partners try to guess the answer by the given clues.

Topics can include:

Vocabulary words/definitions, topics from social studies, science, health, etc., character traits from a story, famous quotes (guess what play or story), formulas (solve the problem), sequencing, etc.

When the partners agree on the answer they return the box to its owners and state, *"We think the answer is ..., because ..."* (giving reason/rationale). The box's owners affirm correctness or state, *"That's a point, our idea was..."* giving the correct answer.

Teams can exchange boxes with several partner teams within a time limit.

NOTES

OTHER *HINTS* FOR COOPERATIVE TEAM LEARNING

After "Start-Up"

Beginning Ground Rules

Ways of "linking"

Individual Accountability

Teacher Monitoring

Some Ways to Debrief

Appreciation Statements

NOTES

AFTER "START-UP"

The teacher needs several ways to link the teammembers so they realize they are in a team and must function and work accordingly.

After the basic ground rules are in place, the teacher or teams can add rules (social skills) as needed. Of course, these must be taught and demonstrated also.

Roles might be added, as necessary and useful toward keeping all teammembers actively involved.

Keeping in mind that with small teams the Ground Rule "Take Turns" usually covers this.

Debriefing plays an important role when teams are getting started. *"How did we do?" "How can we improve?"* These questions and others can be addressed in a short time set aside after each cooperative activity, (closure-summary to a lesson).

BEGINNING RULES
Social Skills - For Start Up

Choose only three or four initially, add on others as needed.

- Quiet voices
- Take turns
- Mistakes are okay
- Stay with your group
- Everyone participates
- Try ideas
- Listen carefully to others
- Ask others for help
- Check with the teacher only when all teammembers do not understand
- Encourage your partner (put-downs not allowed)

- Other: any behavior needed for the team to function

The rules should be short and concise, making them easy for students to remember.

Always include the signal to stop Auditory signal which the students are trained to respond, stop and give the teacher full attention.

WAYS OF "LINKING"

Helping students realize they are part of a team. Choose two or more. The more the better!

√Environment- make sure students can "huddle" together. Sitting side-by-side is best.

√Limit the materials used- one book, pencil, scissors, or paper, etc. per team. Forces the students to sit close and work together.

√One product from the team- Eg. one paper submitted, signed by all.

√Task, activity, divided- between the teammembers and can't be finished without all parts submitted.

√Pass one pencil and paper- around the team, each member must do a part. Assistance and input may be given by other members. This can be considered a Round Robin format.

√Jigsaw materials- each member learns a part to teach the team.

√Team reward- free tickets, bonus points, tallies, stamps, stickers, certificates, etc. If everyone on the team succeeds.

√Setting the goal- criteria for success Both partners' participation is crucial to meeting the goal. The goal may reflect back to the activity (objective) the rules or any part of lesson.

E.g., Turn in paper with 7 out of 10 correct and your team has met the goal...or receive 3 tallies on your Team Card and your team is successful...

Other *HINTS* for Cooperative Team Learning

INDIVIDUAL ACCOUNTABILITY

> **Every student** is responsible for learning the material and being involved.

Choose one or two, the more the better:

√ Administer a short test or quiz, taken individually by the students.

√ Students do the work first, bring work to the group, reach consensus on the answers.

√ Choose students randomly to answer questions studied by the team (while working in small teams or during a class review).

√ Everyone writes, team certifies correctness, staples team papers together, teacher corrects top paper.

√ Teacher monitors, listens and watches as teammembers respond while working in their teams.

√ Assign roles, to keep everyone involved, change roles part-way through the activity, after each problem/question or after 1-2 minutes, to ensure equal involvement.

√ Exit ticket, the teacher writes one or more questions on the board. To leave class the individual hands in the Exit question(s).

√ Teams can earn bonus points, tickets, etc. if all teammembers do well individually.

√ Each teammember uses a different color of ink or crayon from other teammates to show who contributed what information, signing their names in the color used.

√ Follow-up review sheet, done individually.

√ Signing/initialing, questions done by the individual to show involvement and understanding.

TEACHER MONITORING
While teams are working Do Several!

√ **Reinforce** positive group interaction, through immediate praise or rewarding (stamping paper, bonus points, verbal praise, smile, etc.)

√ **Use positive praising** pointing out deficiencies tactfully during debriefing.

√ **Do not intervene** unless absolutely necessary. Allow students to work out their differences.

√ **Avoid giving answers,** learning stops once answers are given. Have teammates check with one another and other teams to search for answers from one another.

√ **Reteach or add to teaching** as necessary.

√ **Reinforce** the use praise/encouragement and partners helping one another to learn.

√ **Determine** what social skills (rules) are mastered and what skills need to be added and taught.

√ **Take verbatim data** to be able to give specific examples during debriefing.

SOME WAYS TO DEBRIEF
What went well, what needs improvement

The most powerful element of cooperative learning and should be included as part of the lesson as the closure and summary.

Plan beforehand specific debriefing questions which directly relate to the lesson. Questions may refer to the:

ACADEMIC OBJECTIVE
(the lesson or task)

TEAM GOAL (criteria for success)

SOCIAL OBJECTIVE and/or TEAM INTERACTION

FUTURE PLANS -academic/social
(suggested by students/teacher)

GROUND RULES

ROLES

The students, with their partners: judge how well they did toward reaching their goal or accomplishing the task. They then discuss and then plan what they will continue or do differently.

Debriefing, summarizing, at the end of a lesson or throughout the lesson. Options can include...

ACADEMIC:
* Ways we accomplished the task were by...
* The answers to the questions are...
* The question / task was difficult because...
* Add yours:

SOCIAL:
* We accomplished our social objective by..
* We kept everyone involved by...
* Ways we encouraged were... by saying...
* We stayed on task by...
* We came to agreement by...

GOAL:
* We did/not meet our goal of... because...
* Ways we met our goal were...
* Ways we could improve are...
* Add yours:

ROLES: (if assigned)
* (role) did /not do the job of ___ by ___
E.g. *"The checker did his /her job of checking for understanding by asking each of us to explain how we arrived at the answer."*

* Ways to improve...
* Another way to...
* We will continue to...
* Add more:

TEAM SHARE ANSWERS:
* When your team has finished, stand, and team share with the next team that stands. Teams cannot just "give" answers, they have to say, *"We think the answer is ___ because ___."*

APPRECIATION STATEMENT TO TEAMMATES:
> Encourages students to use closure and positive feedback to end an activity.

"(Name), you helped me /our team by..."

"____, you did a great job of..."

"____, I appreciated it when..."

"____, you are very good at..."

Add others:

The teacher can distribute, write on the board/overhead, or verbalize debriefing questions before the end of the lesson so those students who finish early will be kept occupied.

Although debriefing forms may be used, oral debriefing should be included as a follow-up to reinforce positive behavior and goal accomplishment as well as putting focus on behaviors/skills which need improvement.

Partner or Team Share to compare answers and give reason and rationale on how answers were reached. This process is highly effective because students receive confirmation that their information is accurate as well as learning different approaches to solving or reaching decisions. *"We/I think the answer is _____ because _____."*

Debriefing need not take longer than 10 minutes. Three to ten minutes set aside can cover a lot of information and reinforce positive behavior. Teams can set academic and/or social goals for future cooperative lessons.

Refer to Debriefing Highlights, pages 59-65

NOTES

Section 6

Ground RULES - Social
Skills

Goals + REWARDS = Feedback

Why ROLES?

THE THREE R'S: RULES - REWARDS - ROLES

After Start-Up: Additional social skills may need to be taught, practiced, and become a <u>rule</u> for the team.

<u>Roles</u> can be introduced as needed and appropriate for the activity.

<u>Rewards</u> can be an effective means of "linking" teammembers, so they see a purpose for working together and accomplishing the <u>goal</u> (criteria for success).

Rewards are the feedback to teams that they are meeting the established <u>goal</u>.

If teams are working well together, a reward system is probably not necessary. Even so, individuals like to "see" a purpose or receive some type of "feedback" which, if handled well, can be the ultimate reward.

Rewards can range from a smile, making tallies on team cards-, to accumulated points,- to grades.

To avoid too much competition between teams, a teacher might want to set up situations so that **every team**, that meets the criteria, <u>goal</u> gets the reward (As opposed to, the <u>first</u> team finished, the team with the <u>best</u> product, etc.).

GROUND RULES and SOCIAL SKILLS

> After choosing 3 or 4 start up **Ground Rules**, and the teams have shown they are following these rules (social skills)...

Observation of the teams while they are working may give you ideas as to what social skills to add, teach, model, or use in the "script" of your directions to the students..

The teacher and/or the students **give a rationale** for the new skill. Now this newly taught and experienced social skill will become a rule. Have the students monitor the skill so it will stay in place. Monitoring can be as simple as placing tallies on their paper every time they "encourage their partner."

BEGINNING SKILLS (Ground RULES) COULD INCLUDE:
Choose 3 or 4 and an **auditory signal to stop**, add other skills later as needed.

- **Quiet voices** (is a must!)
- Take turns
- Everyone participates
- Mistakes are okay
- Stay on task
- Stay with the group
- Try ideas
- Listen carefully to others
- Ask others for help
- Encourage your partner (put-downs not allowed)
- Ask the teacher only if ALL teammembers do NOT understand

Signal to Stop is...   Back Up Signal is ...

OTHER SOCIAL SKILLS COULD INCLUDE:
Teach one at a time <u>after</u> the Ground Rules are in place.

- Listen carefully without interrupting
- Use "I" and "we" when summarizing (as opposed to "you")
- Staying within the time limits
- Reaching agreement / coming to consensus
- Use one another's name
- Praising/Encouraging one another (using affirmations)
- Paraphrasing others' contributions
- Linking this assignment with past learning
- Summarizing information learned
- Checking for understanding
- Seek justification, rationale for answer from others
  (using " because")
- Share orally how to teach/explain information
- Energize the group through constructive humor, ideas,
  suggestions or enthusiasum
- Think of unique ways to remember facts and ideas
- Accept all opinions, ask for rationale *("That's a good point, how
  did you arrive at that ...?")*
- Ask for opinions, *("What do you think?")* add value statements
- Disagree with opinions without criticizing (*"That's a point, my
  idea is ..."*)
- Ask your partner's opinion before offering your ideas

C&M Education Consultants

NOTES

GOALS + REWARDS = FEEDBACK

How often do students set goals for themselves? Or, when do students learn to set goals?

Just as adults set goals for themselves, *"I want to save $100. to buy..."* Goal setting is a life-skill that students should be encouraged and guided toward implementation at an early age.

In a cooperative lesson a goal(s) can be established by the team, teacher, or input from the class.

Examples of goal setting:
"Your goal today, for your team to be successful, is for your team to improve your base "pretest" score.

"Decide on a goal for your team for today's assignment, and how you know you have accomplished the goal. Write this down on the bottom of today's assignment."

Rewards are assigned so teams can see the "purpose" in working together. Rewards are also "invitations" to encourage students to participate.

Rewards can also be considered "feedback" to students so they know how well they are doing.

Often when students do not want to participate, or are not working well together, it is because they don't understand the "purpose" or know the *rationale* behind the activity. Rewards serve as a "purpose" and the feedback for being involved.

Rewards are the feedback that the team goal was accomplished.
E.g., *"Your team met its goal of getting five out of seven answers correct. Your team earns 1 bonus point."* or *"Your team met the goal of using encouragement, give your partner a high-five!"*

Rewards can be linked to the goal (criteria for success). They may be awarded for accomplishing the social and/or academic objective (activity).
E.g., *"If you earn five tallies for encouraging in your team, your team will be successful."*

Rewards can be as simple as praise or tallies on a Team Card to grades, bonus points, free time, and skipped assignments, etc.

Record keeping for rewards should be kept simple so that the teacher does not become overwhelmed by the "bookkeeping" element.

Rewards should be awarded to all members of the team which meet the criteria, not individuals. Rewards should also be as immediate as possible, as they are a positive means of "feedback" to students.

Avoid, *"The first team finished, gets to..."* or *"The team with the best ...gets to..."* This promotes competition between teams and often a feeling of rivalry. Statements such as, *"All teams that finish will get to..."* gives the impression that, *"We all have an opportunity to accomplish the goal!"*

Are rewards necessary? If every student in a classroom is working well, enjoys school, has appropriate behavior, and works in a team...no! But, feedback to students is important, and what better way to give positive, specific feedback than with praise, a tally, bonus point, or a stamp on the team paper! This is appropriate for all levels, secondary included.

In junior high or high school levels, some teachers tape manila envelopes to the side of team desks (Rebecca Wolle, Linda McJunkin and team). When each class enters, the teams get their Team Cards, etc. from the envelope to place on their team desk.

Pat Canon, physics teacher, has cut 9" X 11" boards from shower stall material. He drilled a 1" hole in one corner, and has attached cup hooks under the outside lip of the team desks.

The boards hang on the hooks under the lip of the desk. When the teacher requests a team answer or response, the students use Dry Erase Markers, or grease pens for writing team answers and keeping track of <u>team marks or tallies</u> for correct responses.

Old socks can serve as erasers as well as holding the Dry Erase Markers. The open end of the sock can slip through the second hole drilled in the board, keeping the marker and board easy to reach when needed.

> <u>Option:</u> Make slate boards by applying chalkboard Contac paper or dry erase Contac paper to heavy cardstock or railroad board and cut to desired size. Students can Partner Share their answers, give reason for their answer and erase if partners agree.

When the team has arrived at an answer, the teacher can request the teams to hold up their team board, or individually check the board answers as the teacher is monitoring. Thereby the teacher eliminates the correcting of additional papers.

The teacher gives those teams who have correct answers, tallies or points on their board, the team records and hands these to the teacher as they exit.

Exit Quiz - Ticket
For <u>individual accountability</u> to check that individuals understand the material, or to get an individual grade; the teacher can write one to four questions on the chalkboard or overhead on the subject material just covered.

The students, <u>individually</u> (by themselves), write their answer(s) to the question(s), and hand the teacher their answers as they exit. The teacher can use this information to assign an individual grade or use for reference.

REWARDS FOR ELEMENTARY:

- phone call to parents
- happy grams
- teams of the week / day
- daily announcements
- display team work
- applause, hug, smile, etc.
- teams helpers for the day
- lunch with the teacher / principal
- gum chewing
- choose item from prize box (pencil eraser, bookmark, etc.)
- reader to other students / principal
- free time / recess
- play a special game
- extra P.E., art, music, computer time
- special day if all teams succeed: Hawaiian Day, T-shirt Day, Stuffed Animal Day,etc.
- keep class mascot on team table (stuffed animal)
- stars, stickers, stamps (in multicolored ink)
- snacks, treats
- grab bag (food coupons, little toys, pencils, toothbrushes, etc.)
- points earned toward prize, or grab bag items
- skip test or homework assignment
- popcorn party
- AV treat
- bonus points (which could be used to raise a grade or average)
- extra credit
- grade
- other:

REWARDS FOR MIDDLE SCHOOL:

- notes mailed home to parents
- phone calls to parents
- happy grams (mailed to parents)
- team(s) of the week
- display work
- applause
- free pass
- free time
- helpers
- early lunch
- no assignment
- no homework
- skip test
- extra credit
- popcorn
- computer time
- daily announcements recognition
- library passes
- AV treat
- special day if all teams succeed
- stickers
- snacks
- ice cream
- tokens for school store
- chance for drawing (food coupons, pencils)
- bonus points toward grade
- grade
- other:

NOTES:

REWARDS FOR HIGH SCHOOL:

- notes mailed home to parents
- phone calls to parents
- newsletter recognition
- team picture displayed
- stickers
- snacks
- ice cream, treats
- free passes
- AV treat
- grade
- bonus points (can go toward grade change)
- extra credit
- video game tokens
- library passes
- free time
- special privileges
- computer time
- no assignment coupon
- skip a test
- no homework coupon
- early lunch
- happy grams mailed home
- display work
- other:

Note: Free food coupons for your teams to earn can be obtained, no obligation, from your local, national, fast food restaurants and pizza parlors, just by asking the Store Manager for them!

If Roles are used, the purpose of the role assignment is two-fold:

> √ To keep all teammembers actively involved and participating throughout the task or assignment.
> √ To teach/review a social skill and give teammembers an opportunity to experience and/or monitor the social skill.

Roles Should Be:
√ Carefully selected for **each** cooperative activity.

√ The role should **fit the activity** so there is **continuous involvement** for ALL teammembers.

√ **Switched** after a designated time, number of sentences, number of problems, etc. Teammembers can experience **equal opportunity** with a role or responsibility and **keep** everyone **equally involved**.

Roles need not be:
√ Assigned if they are **not appropriate** for the activity.

√ Assigned if they do **not** keep all teammembers **involved** throughout the activity.

√ Assigned if teams are small and a Rule or Simple Structure keeps teammembers involved:
E.g., Rule- Take Turns
   Simple Structure- Round Robin

Take into Consideration When Assigning Role
When first introducing cooperative learning and teaching or reviewing the Ground Rules, a teacher might consider **not** assigning roles. Role assignment entails additional direction-giving and the teaching of the role and its responsibility.

After the teams are beginning to work in their teams and know how to work together, the teacher may see a need for role assignments. At this time the lesson will include the "review" of a social skill and less direction giving will be necessary.

When introducing a role it is necessary to **teach** the role and its responsibility just as you would **teach and model** the Ground Rules, social skills. Do **not** assume if you assign a "checker" role that all the students know or understand this role the same as the teacher interprets the responsibility of the "checker."

Some roles have "scripts." It is important that the students have some input as to what these scripts might be and the purpose of the role.
E.g., *"Today in our activity you will take turns being a checker. The checker's responsibility is to make sure your partner understands how to arrive at the answer."*

"To make sure your partner understands, what are some things you could ask your partner to make sure s/he do understand?"

The teacher writes on the board or overhead suggestions:
"One thing I do not want you to ask your partner is 'Do you understand?' Why?"

"It is too easy to say 'Yes,' without proving you do understand."

The teacher reviews scripts suggested, which might include:
"Show me..." "Explain to me..." "Go through the steps to solve..." "How did you...?"

These scripts can be distributed on cards so they may be referenced when doing the role with a partner.

All Activities Do Not Need Roles, Therefore, Do Not Assign Roles

Make sure the role fits the activity. I have often observed students who were assigned a "generic" role where the student had nothing to do until the end of the activity when it was their turn to do their job (role).

Often, when roles are assigned students assume that if they do **not** have a particular role assignment they are not to be involved until it is their turn to do their job (role).

Therefore, in many cases, roles can actually **lower** the involvement instead of increasing it.

This often happens when teachers incorporate a role which has little responsibility and do **not** have students **switch** or rotate role assignments throughout a lesson/activity.

Roles Should Be Rotated

throughout the activity, giving all students the opportunity to keep equally involved as well as learning the role and its responsibility.
E.g., *"The person on the right (or: red dot) will be the Reader. You will read the question and answer it."*

"The person on the left (or: blue dot) is the Writer. You will assist the reader if necessary and write the answer."

"You will change roles/jobs after each question."

NOT:

"One of you is the Reader, you read everything. Your partner is the Materials Handler, you get the materials needed."

One person might read for fifteen minutes and the Materials Handler puts the book away! This is **not** equal involvement.

Rotating roles will assist in developing and strengthening the reading and writing skills of the teammembers. A partner who does **not** enjoy reading, but who would benefit from the practice will only read every other sentence, paragraph or page.
E.g., *"I don't like to write, but I only have to write every other answer, not all the answers!" "I think I can handle that!"*

Assign the Roles When Students are in Their Teams

Often teachers make the mistake of giving directions and role assignments, **then** placing students into teams. The students are confused as to what their responsibility is and therefore time is lost in reexplanation and discussions.

Roles can lengthen the directions to an activity, but in some cases, roles can shorten direction giving.

If an activity has multiple steps and direction giving would be lengthy, give each partner a "step" as a role for which they are responsible. This could be in a written format:

Partner I: Read the...
Partner II: Write the...

Partner I: Solve the...
Partner II: Record the...

The Same Role Can Be Shared Between Teammembers

Example:
*"You are **both** Encouragers, your role is to encourage and ask your partner to share ideas."*

Scripts could include:
"What do you think?" "Tell me more!"
"Good idea." "How did you arrive at that answer?"

ROLE REVIEW:

Roles are assigned to keep **all** teammembers **involved and included** throughout an activity. If a Ground Rule or Simple Structure already does this, role assignment are **not** necessary.

Roles, after being established for the lesson, can be teacher assigned, randomly assigned or chosen by the teammembers themselves. The latter might be avoided with younger children, least they disagree on who does what job, taking valuable team work time for deciding a role assignment.

The roles should be **taught** and **reviewed** until the **students** understand the responsibility of each role. Using limited roles is helpful

Make sure the roles are **appropriate for the activity** and that you are not giving a role assignment which is unrelated to the task being done by the team.
E.g., Assigning a recorder and there is little or no written work involved in this lesson/task.

Debrief the roles at the conclusion of the lesson getting student input as to how well they performed their role when it was their turn.

Often teacher omit debriefing a role, yet after a team activity might remark, *"I didn't hear very much encouragement and I assigned them roles of Encourager!"*

The debriefing session is the time to reflect on this and remind the students of the role, how they might improve or what they can continue doing.

Write down this feedback and in the next activity be sure to include the same role to reinforce the desired skill/responsibility which it enhances.

Roles might be placed in two categories

Roles that do a job or task.
E.g., Reader, Writer.

Roles that have scripts.
E.g., Checker, Encourager/Praiser.

Initially, Job Cards, are often placed on team desks (at all levels), to assist and remind the students of their job or script. E.g., You are the Checker, you are to make sure your partner understands by asking:
"Explain to me..." or "Tell me how you arrived at the answer for..."

Author's note:
Due to the large number of teachers and lessons which I have observed, I have opinions about roles:

Roles if not appropriate for the activity, allow students to sit and **wait** to do their role (so much so as to allow "off-task" behavior) Switching or rotating roles frequently is a good option to this unequal involvement.

Also, I notice roles being assigned when the lesson **did not need** roles; thus, using direction-giving time unnecessarily for role explanation and assignment.

ROLES COULD INCLUDE

Reminder: Do not use roles if they **do not fit** the lesson/task.

Reader: someone who reads the material outloud to the team.

Writer: records the best answers from the team, gets all teammembers to sign the paper and turns it in to the teacher.

Materials Handler: Gets any materials or equipment needed by the group, keeps track of them and puts them away. (Another role can be giving in addition to this role or the partners share the role; one doing the job before the activity, the second partner puts the materials away.)

◆ **Encourager:** Watches to make sure that everyone is participating and invites reluctant or silent members to participate. With such statements as: "___, what do you think?" or "___, can you add to this?" (This role can be shared. Each partner gives one another encouragement and gives one another a tally to keep record of encouragements given).

◆ **Checker:** Checks on the comprehension or learning of the teammembers by asking them to explain or summarize the material learned or discussed.
Statements could include:
"___, explain how we arrived at this answer."

◆ **Praiser:** Helps members feel good about their contributions to the group by telling them how helpful they are. This role and the role of **Encourager** may be assigned to combat "put-downs."

Noise Monitor: Uses a non-verbal signal to remind teammembers to lower the noise level. (Not necessary to have one in every team. Three per class assigned).

◆ **Summarizer:** Summarizes the material so that team members can check it again.
Statements could include: *"Most of us think...," "It seems like...," "It sounds like we want..."*

Timekeeper: Helps keep the teams working toward their "target" time for accomplishing the objective/activity. (One person for the class).

◆ **Questioner:** Asks pertinent questions to involve others and move toward summary.
Questions could be: *"What do you think...?" "Would you like...?" "Who would like to...?"*

◆ **Paraphraser:** Retells what they understood another teammember share, without taking notes or using the exact words.

◆ **Idea giver:** Contributes ideas toward the team activity.
Contributions could include:
"I think...," "Maybe...," "My idea is...," "Another way is to...," "We could...," etc.

◆ **Linker:** Is assigned to encourage students to "link" information from past learning to the current activity.

◆ **Agreer:** Is a role which may be assigned to an individual/team when having difficulty reaching consensus.

◆ **Asker for help:** A role assigned, with a script, if individual/team is having difficulty asking for assistance.
"___,could you show me how to...," "___,I need some help with...,"

Key: ◆ = **Role uses scripts.**

57

NOTES

DEBRIEFING HIGHLIGHTS

Section 7

DEBRIEFING
Powerful tool, but often left undone.

Due to lack of time, lack of questions to ask, or lack of variety in approaches, debriefing is often *omitted* from a cooperative lesson.

Debriefing is the most *powerful* component of the cooperative learning structure.

Debriefing can change behaviors, work habits, enhance learning, and affirm understanding and accuracy.

Closure and summarization are components of debriefing. Review can take place here as well as what went well in the activity and what can be improved.

Goals can be set by the teams for improvement or what they might want to work toward accomplishing in the next activity.

Teams "buy-in" to their learning when they are allowed to give input. What safer place for input but in a small team environment?

DEBRIEFING   FORMAT
Debriefing time can be **renamed** by the teacher and/ or the students:
"Wrap-up," "Talk it Over," "Recap," "Reflecting Time," "Interview," or whatever applies to the cooperative activity or task and the age of the students.

Debriefing can be done individually, within the teams, between teams, whole class, or a combination of these. (It does not always have to be done with the teacher as the facilitator). It is the summary or closing of the lesson

Debriefing can be done in a written format or with oral feedback or a combination of both.

Note: For start-up, if a written format is used, the teacher should also include some time for oral interaction as well so teams can "hear" positive feedback and learn from the examples of others how to improve, not only their social interaction, but how to be more productive with their academic objective as well.

Teammembers should remain in their teams during debriefing, and not "break up" and return to other desks or room formations.

Individual teams can debrief in a Partner Share format: *"Turn to your partner and discuss..."*

NOTE:
Debriefing with teammembers can be very valuable. Teams can reflect on their goals, write team goals for future reference, celebrate their successes, and give their team chant or handshake (if appropriate!). They can **not** do this easily if they are <u>not</u> in their original working teams during debriefing.

OR...debrief between teams in a Team Share format: *"Go to another team and explain..."*

OR...in an Interview format, have the partners question one another or another team on specific, preassigned questions which reflect back on the lesson/activity: *"Partner (name), share the three steps you (we) went through to solve..."*

OR...the teacher can wander from team to team, interact, question, discuss, and receive feedback: *"Explain to me how you arrived at..."*

DECIDE   BEFOREHAND
Have 1-4 questions preplanned which reflect back on the activity (objective or lesson), social skills (rules), roles (if assigned), the goal (criteria for success) or the finished product (if applicable).

Questions may be written on the board, overhead, distributed, appear on the bottom or back of a worksheet, or given orally by the teacher.

Preassigned questions give closure and summarize the activity. Often the target time runs out, and there is **not** sufficient time for oral feedback. Closure of the lesson has taken place within the teams through these preassigned questions.

FEEDBACK FROM THE TEACHER

As the teams are working: the teacher is wandering, monitoring, eavesdropping, and assisting if necessary.

Immediate, positive feedback is also given at this time. Feedback comes in the form of praise, encouragement, awarding bonus points, tallies/stamps on the project, paper or Team Card, etc.

The teams and individual students have been given immediate feedback throughout the activity from the teacher. If there is not enough time during oral debriefing for further teacher feedback, it has taken place while the teams were working.

In traditional classrooms the students often have to wait for their project/paper to be corrected, graded, and returned to "see" teacher feedback.

In a Cooperative Team Learning environment, feedback, reinforcement, and encouragement are ongoing. It comes not only from the teacher, but from teammembers as well.

Is it any surprise that self esteem is raised, new friendships are developed, and a greater liking for school is enhanced through this teaching structure?

WHEN SOME TEAMS FINISH EARLY

When teams finish before others, they may be kept occupied by working on the preassigned debriefing questions, or a "sponge" activity added to the lesson.

SUGGESTIONS

Submit questions focused toward the academic and social skills involved in the team's activity or lesson. Because debriefing activities direct questions to the students, they provide a natural integration of communication and thinking skills.

Students must think about what has just occurred, what they have learned, how their team functioned, and/or how they themselves behaved within the team.

They should then communicate these thoughts to others, and set measurable goals for their teams for improvement. These can be written, submitted to the teacher, and redistributed to the teams to review for the next cooperative activity.

DEBRIEFING

May be general or specific. The questions are a reflection of any of the following in the lesson: social skills academic objective, roles, goal (criteria for success), or the finished product.
Example:
   A general academic question could be to, "Name one new thing learned during the lesson."
   A more specific academic debriefing question would be to ask each student: What s/he did to help the team learn the information.

   A general social skill question may be to identify: How the team worked together to complete the activity.
   A more specific debriefing question would be to ask each student: What s/he did to help the team complete the activity.

IMPORTANT FACTORS
Consider these when planning debriefing activities-

√ A debriefing activity should <u>immediately</u> follow each cooperative lesson.

√ The activity should take only 3-10 minutes.

√ For variety, a debriefing activity should <u>vary</u> in <u>format</u>: Sometimes within the team, teams with other teams, at other times whole class debriefing.

√ Have the students "turn to your partner" and come up with a <u>team</u> response on occasion.

√ Get students' opinions <u>first</u>. The teacher gives input and observations <u>last.</u> If the teacher shares his/her opinions first, what will the students have left to share? Or, if their opinions differ from the teacher's, will they speak up?

√ Give specific examples and data, be positive, *"I noticed in this team _____,"*

√ Avoid generalities, *"You all did a good job!"*

√ Offer specific changes which need to be made, and have the students decide how (by teams) they can make necessary changes and how they will be able to observe/monitor the changes.

OTHER IDEAS
Ranking-
Have the teams decide on a scale, 1-5, how their team did in accomplishing the social and academic objective, meeting the goal, finishing the product, or other questions relating to the activity.

5	4	3	2	1
Very well				Not very well

Thumbs / Pencils Up
Questions with "yes" or "no" responses can be asked, and answers can be solicited individually or by team consensus. ("Pencils Up" for older students).
E.g., *"Thumbs up if you..."*
      "Thumbs up if your team..."

Whip
Ask a <u>summarizing question</u> for each student to offer a short, concise opinion or response.

Starting at one side of the classroom, "whip" through all the students' responses in order of their seating arrangement.

Students will give their response quickly. The teacher will be non-judgmental, acknowledging all responses in the affirmative.

A student may say "pass," meaning they need more "think time," and the teacher will return to them later.

Example for social skill objective:
"Share one way you encouraged your partner during this activity/lesson."

Example for academic objective:
"Share an idea of how you might apply what you learned today to..."

Example for goal:
"Share the goal you set for this activity and how it was/was not met."

FEEDBACK CARDS
At the close of the activity, teammates write down their response to the lesson. Cards (3X5) can be used, for the students' open-ended reactions.
E.g.,
• *"List ways your partner helped your team accomplish the goal."*
• *"Give examples of what you might do differently next time."*
• *"Which question/problem was most difficult? Why?"*

These questions may be done individually or in teams. However, the teacher may ask students to respond to a specific question or directions such as:

"Write down the number of times you gave encouragement to another team-member and what it was you said."

Or *"Write down one new idea you learned today which came from this lesson."*

Or *"Write down, as a team, how the information you learned today is related to information you have learned from (the last lesson, last week's assignment, yesterday's assignment, past learning, etc.)*
Refer to: SENTENCE STARTERS, this page

> Feedback cards are collected by the teacher and used for reference, planning, and goal setting.

HUDDLING/ PARTNER SHARE
Teammembers put their heads together to discuss specific topics such as;
"One way our team worked to accomplish its goal today is..."

Or *"The most interesting part of this _____ assignment was..."*

Or *"If you were the teacher, how would you change this activity?"*

Allow a minute or so of private thinking time before beginning the team/class discussion.
Refer to: SENTENCE STARTERS -this page

DEBRIEFING FORM
A prewritten debriefing sheet with 1-5 specific questions is given to each team or individuals. The questions should lend themselves to short responses.

At the end of the response time, the teams can share these with one another. Or if they are done individually, they can be shared within their team. The teacher can collect these responses for feedback, future reference, and goal setting.
Refer to: DEBRIEFING FORMS, pp.143 & 144

SENTENCE STARTERS
To avoid asking the same questions during each debriefing session, sentence starters for individual or team response can be used.

SENTENCE STARTERS FOR DEBRIEFING

I(WE) LEARNED...

I(WE) REALIZED THAT...

I(WE) CHANGED MY(OUR) OPINION ABOUT...

I'M(WE'RE) BEGINNING TO WONDER...

I(WE) NOTICED...

I(WE) WAS (WERE) SURPRISED...

I(WE) REDISCOVERED...

I(WE) WAS(WERE) REMINDED OF...

I(WE) HOPE THAT...

I(WE) WAS(WERE) PLEASED...

I(WE) FELT THAT...

IT WOULD HAVE BEEN BETTER IF...

NEXT TIME I (WE)...

WHAT I (WE) LEARNED TODAY RELATES TO...
Add others...

Teams can Team Share with another team and offer solutions and suggestions.

TEAM CARDS and FORMS

As teams are working, a 3X5, 4X6 card, or Team Card/Form, can be placed on each team table.

As the teams are working appropriately, the teacher puts "tallies" or "stamps" on the card to reinforce the positive behavior or work observed.

The teacher whispers the behavior to reinforce the team and so other teams may "overhear" how to earn "tallies" or "stamps" (which might go toward the team goal or class privileges).

Later instead of whispering the behavior, a feedback Form can be used which lists the type of behavior or expectation for the team. The teacher-observer makes tallies or stamps by the word or picture on the Form so not to interrupt the team.

E.g., The feedback Form might read:

Team name:
Taking turns: ||
Quiet voices: |||
Encouraging: |
Other...

Refer to: Appendix pages 152 & 153

Tallies are made by the teacher, or the teacher can instruct teams to make tallies on Team Cards as appropriate.

The tallies/stamps or whatever the teacher issues can count toward: Bonus points to raise a grade, or a privilege (computer time, skip a homework assignment, etc.).

Or as simple as: The team can celebrate earning __X__ number of tallies by giving their team handshake and rap!

These are goals for the teams to try to attain. The "reward," when the goal is reached, must meet the level of need of the teammembers.

APPRECIATION STATEMENT
Given at the end of a cooperative lesson

Each teammember is directed to give a compliment (affirmation) individually to his/her teammate(s) about how s/he helped the team accomplish the task.

The students may volunteer to share some of the positive statements said to them. By sharing orally, others may hear "scripts" for appropriate affirmations. (an alternative for "put-downs")

If students are having difficulty with compliments/affirmations, give them "starter statements" until they can comfortably initiate statements.

Students should be instructed as to "feeling tone" so as not to sound phony or insincere. Before long these statements become natural, comfortable, and sincere with use.

APPRECIATION STARTERS
"I want to thank you for ..."
"I appreciate it when ..."
"(Name), you really helped me when..."
"Thank you, I think you are..."
"I felt good when..."
"I liked it when..."
"It was good working with you because..."

Reminder: Encourage students to state the person's name to whom they are speaking.
For older students: If the students and/or teacher are not comfortable initially with affirmation statements, an alternative might be:
"Write how or what your partner contributed today... (pause long enough for them to write), share this with your partner."

Procedure for debriefing -review

Debriefing can be a very **powerful** element of a teacher's cooperative lesson. It can be used to **correct** and **reinforce** not only <u>behavior,</u> but academic objectives as well.

1. Decide *beforehand* , specific statements for *academic* and *social skill* objectives, questions that reflect back to the lesson itself (not "generic" questions).

2. Write statements on the *board* or *distribute* copies or *verbalize* the statements to be debriefed. These prearranged questions can keep those teams that finish early occupied.

3. After the team task is completed or time is up, students *review* the debriefing statements. They respond individually, with their *partner ,* or share their team *responses* with another team.

4. The teacher can request *individual* or team responses in *oral* or *written* format.

5. The teacher can go to each *team* or ask for *class* responses.

6. Teams can set *goals* for their next team activity.

7. The teacher summarizes *last !* giving *positive, specific ,* *examples,*

8. Collect Feedback Cards and Debriefing Sheets for *reference* and *future* *planning .*

9. Take *five* minutes to write a short *summary or evaluation* of the lesson for *goal setting .*

10. An *appreciation (affirmation)* *statement* , should be included , (each partner saying a compliment to their partner),as the ending activity of a Cooperative Team lesson.

NOTES

WHY COOPERATIVE TEAMS OFTEN DO NOT WORK WELL

Section 8

WHY COOPERATIVE TEAMS OFTEN DO NOT WORK WELL

This section addresses why teams often do not work well. These observations have been compiled from hundreds of teachers doing cooperative lessons:

- ◆ Team Size
- ◆ Team Composition
- ◆ Classroom Arrangement
- ◆ Trustbuilding-Bonding
- ◆ Ground Rules
- ◆ Social Skills
- ◆ Limited Materials
- ◆ Goal
- ◆ Reward-Feedback
- ◆ Debriefing
- ◆ Roles
- ◆ Classroom Management Techniques

Remember:
The following are all "caution" signals...

◆ TEAM SIZE

Teams too large, the students do not have the necessary **social skills** to include everyone effectively.

Larger teams cut down individual interaction:

"95% of how we learn is teaching someone else, 80% is experiencing it personally, and 70% is when it is discussed."

Teams of two are most ideal for high level of success and maximum interaction.

◆ TEAM COMPOSITION

What criteria went into putting the teams together?

> **Avoid:** Random selection and students selecting their own teams.

Include girl-boy combinations. Select teams with diversity to balance deficiencies.

If teams are not carefully teacher-selected, some combinations may experience difficulty.

◆ CLASSROOM ARRANGEMENT

Partners should be sitting side-by-side, facing the teacher.

> **Avoid:** • work being upside down, • partners facing, • two desks apart or across a table • backs to the front or the teacher.

When backs are to the teacher or partners are across from one another, problems can arise.

◆ ☆ TRUSTBUILDING-BONDING

If students are placed into teams and are expected to begin an activity, to interact with one another and possibly make a mistake, they have to build trust.

> When trust or bonding is lacking, students might fold their arms, refuse to work with their partner or in a team , or move their desks apart.

A bonding activity might have to occur each time the teams are physically separated.
E.g., If they move their desks apart and are not sitting side-by-side, **or** if several days have passed without being involved in teamwork.

◆ GROUND RULES

Short, concise, observable <u>behaviors.</u>

Often the rules are shared with the students but not taught, modeled or applied.

Teach, model, and give feedback. Do not assume that even high school students can take turns during an activity without guidelines.

> **Avoid:**
> √ Lengthy rules, which are difficult to remember.
>
> √ Putting in the negative, ("No Put Downs " Use instead, "Encourage Your Partner)".
>
> √ Rules which are not teachable, measurable behaviors: **Not**, Be kind, cooperate, be polite, etc.

◆ SOCIAL SKILL

A social skill should be included in each lesson, even if the teams are following the Ground Rules. Teams need to be reminded of or taught a new social skill for each lesson.

The social skill should fit and compliment the activity/lesson. The skill should be **monitored** by the teacher and/or the students so the behavior will be reinforced and stay in place.

✦AUDITORY SIGNAL TO STOP

Have an auditory Signal and **teach** what it means. Many teachers do not use their signal effectively to regain control of their class before continuing.

This is essential to have classroom control. Often educators do not *teach* the "stop" signal, assuming the students know what it is and what it means.

A long pause, with the teacher standing quietly and waiting, should follow the Signal. Until everyone's attention is on the teacher, s/he should **not** continue.

⊕LIMITED MATERIALS

Gives the message, *"We have to do this together. I have to wait for you and make sure you understand."*

If materials are shared/limited, it is important that students are not allowed to use their own materials. They will frequently leave their partner behind if they can use their own book/paper and read or work ahead.

✦ESTABLISHING THE GOAL

With the students. What do the teams need to do to be successful?

This is often left undone, assuming the students know what the teacher expects. Students need to strive toward reaching and setting goals.

They will be more willing to work toward the goal when they can see /experience the immediate feedback for accomplishing the preestab-ished goal.

Students understand the term "goal." There are "goals" in sports: *"Run over that line and it is six points." "Kick the ball into the net and it is a point." "Throw the ball through the hoop and it is 1-3 points."*

Goals are set when doing a job: *"Make this many sales and you will receive..." "Finish this project before this date and you will receive.."*

We need to allow students to experience goals in school and in the classroom.
E.g., *"Your team will be successful if your team completes..." "Get three tallies and you have met the goal for today."*

Therefore, students will "buy in" to the purpose and rationale more readily for a lesson or assignment if the goal is *in place* and *attainable*.

✦FEEDBACK - REWARD

How do the teams know if they are doing well, are on target, meeting the goal?

Teachers should have a system to set a lesson goal(s), and a way to show students they have succeeded, for celebration.

E.g., *"You have met the goal of completing the study sheet within the Target Time. Give your partner your handshake and, do your team rap."*

RATIONALE PURPOSE

Do the students understand the *reason-purpose*, of the lesson and how what they are learning might be applied to other learning or experiences?

Students often share, *"This is boring." "Stupid!" "Dumb!"* etc.

Translated: They do not understand the purpose of the activity/assignment.

Review with the students, *"Share with your partner the purpose of this activity."*

"Why do I have you Partner Share (Team Share) these questions?"

Allow the students to arrive at the reason-rationale instead of the teacher "telling" his/her purpose.

⊕✦▼ DEBRIEFING

Difficulties which often occur.
- It is often omitted or slighted.

- Too many "Yes/No" questions.

- Too many individual questions in opposition to team responses, ideas, and suggestions.

- A format which is overused.

- Lack of variety in summarizing techniques.

- Not a smooth transition between the cooperative activity and debriefing. Often negative discipline occurs.

- Questions asked when partners are seated apart from one another.

✳ROLES

What often happens-

√ Additional directions are necessary due to explanation and assigning of roles. Students tire or become confused with the lengthy directions of the lesson, the social skill, the goal and the roles.

√ Students forgetting their role/responsibility, needing reexplanation.

√ Students not involved, waiting their turn to perform their job/role.

√ Assigning roles before putting students into teams; students forgetting their role or arguing over responsibilities.

√ Some roles give more responsibility than others, allowing some students to "withdraw."

If roles are assigned:

• There should be equal involvement.

• Have roles switch after __X__ minutes or after a predesignated number of problems/questions accomplished.

• Assign roles if it cuts down on direction giving.

Decide beforehand if "Taking Turns" or "Round Robin" would be a better option to role assignments, which reduces direction- giving.

CLASSROOM MANAGEMENT TECHNIQUES

In addition to those mentioned:
- ✓ Auditory Signal to Stop

- ✓ Setting a Goal with the students

- ✓ Making sure students have a clear understanding of the rationale-purpose of the lesson/assignment.

Keep in mind the following:

✳CHECKING FOR UNDERSTANDING

How is the teacher checking to make sure all teams understand the instructions or information?

Often a teacher gives directions (assuming they are clear), and then says, *"Get started on this assignment."*

Assuming all of the students interpreted the directions identically...
The teams are now beginning to get into arguments or discussions because partners do not agree on the directions!

OR: A teacher gives the instructions and asks, *"Are there any questions?"*

What student is going to humiliate themselves by shooting his/her hand into the air and admit in front of all his/her peers:

Partner Share would be a good option for checking that everyone understands:

"Share with your partner the directions for..., when you and your partner agree, Team Stand quietly."

Assigning jobs...
But, by not being specific as to who does what job within the team, students become confused or may argue about their responsibility.

NOT THIS:
"One of you will read the question, your partner will write the answers."

THIS:
*"The partner on the **right**, raise your hand. (pause) You will read the questions."*

*"Partner on the **left**, raise your hand. (pause) You will write the answer."*

"Switch jobs after each question."

This takes the guesswork out of who is to do what job and possible conflicts between partners.

◆**TARGET TIME** should be assigned. As a study skill, students need to know the parameters of an activity.

Assigning a target time gives the message to the students: "We need to get down to work, stay on task, and we'll accomplish our goal."

When assigning the Target Time, point to the clock and say, *"You have 15 minutes to do this activity or until 1:15 , (or when the big hand is on three)."*

It is a good idea to help pace the teams by giving them a Warning Time: *"You have three minutes to wind things up."*

✳ TEAMS SHARE
Initially, for classroom control, the teacher should designate which teams will Team Share with whom. This can be done with hand signals from the teacher:
"This team shares with this team," (Gesturing).

OR:
Drop colored/lettered cards on the team tables. They find the team with the matching card to Team Share.

OR:
If teams are in diads/table teams, they can Team Share with the team across from them.

> **NOTE:**
> Physically moving to another position in the classroom to Team Share is an *energizer* for the partners...
> ...But, if not controlled and monitored it can cause a management problem.

✳ TEAM STAND
√ Directions such as, *"Stand **quietly** behind your chairs,"* reminds the teams as to appropriate behavior.

√ Questions with **limited responses** are best for Team Stand.

With limited responses, the teams can be seated within seconds after hearing their idea mentioned.

With unlimited answers, there is a possibility of every team responding. This drags out the process.

√ **Avoid** questions which might take several minutes for teams to come to agreement.
E.g., One team might reach consensus in one minute and stand. Other teams might take two-three minutes, and team number One is standing "patiently" for several minutes.

TEACHER MONITORING:
The teacher's role is to be *constantly monitoring,* **giving feedback,** *questioning, and observing teams* -not sitting at the desk correcting assignments or making lesson plans!

If the teacher is monitoring and giving feedback, will there be a need to hand-in all guided practice assignments?

Probably not, especially if teams Team Share with three other teams to check for accuracy, understanding, and teaching one another. The teacher will observe how well individuals understand concepts.

S/he can make future plans from these observations; reteach, review, assign more guided practice, quiz now, etc.

Evaluate your cooperative learning team structure and activities. If there are any difficulties, walk through each of the points mentioned in this section.

If you decide to make changes, change only **one** thing at a time. If teams are still having difficulty, allow some **adjustment time** to pass before making the next change.

KEY:

✳ refer to: ROLES, pages 54-57

✳ refer to: SIMPLE STRUCTURES, pages 33-39

▼ refer to: DEBRIEFING, pages 18, 19, 44, 45

◆ refer to: GOALS+REWARDS   pages 51-53

☆ refer to: TRUSTBUILDING-BONDING, pages 7, 13, 14, 27-29

◆ refer to: STRUCTURING THE CLASS, pages 6-19

✜ refer to: OTHER "HINTS"   pages 43-45

NOTES

MOST FREQUENT DIFFICULTIES IN
COOPERATIVE LEARNING

Section 9

NOTES

When teachers share difficulties they experience with Cooperative Learning, the following are the concerns which are most frequently mentioned:

√ Students not working well together in teams.

√ Students not able to come to agreement.

√ Teams being too noisy.

√ Some students unwilling to work in a team.

√ Cooperative learning takes too much time.

√ The student(s) no one want(s) in their team.

Included in this section are possible solutions and suggestions which teachers have found to be useful and successful.

Students Not Working Well Together in Teams

How large are the teams?
The major reason that students have difficulty working together is team size.

Often teams are too large, and teammembers usually do not have the necessary social skills to work together successfully.

When teachers cut-back to teams of two, they have experienced a high level of success, less "policing," and more "on task" behavior from the teammembers.

If only one or two teams are having difficulty, including teams of two:
Assign these teams as "Observers" to go to other "exemplary" working teams to take data/observe, and give feedback to their partner(s). They will discuss together how/what they might do to make their team work more compatibly.
Refer to: SIMPLE STRUCTURES -Observer, page 29

Trustbuilding-Bonding
How much bonding was done within the team prior to this activity?

Even if it is one team, this team might need additional "bonding" activities necessary to help them feel comfortable together.

E.g., *While I am taking roll, share with your partner your favorite..."*

If students are pulling their desks away from their partner, backs to one another and arms folded, this is a good sign that more bonding might possibly be a solution.
Refer to: TRUSTBUILDING-BONDING ACTIVITIES, pages 27-29

What is the goal or purpose?
Often, if the students refuse to work together, or are saying things such as:
"Why are we doing this?" "This is stupid!"

What they might actually be thinking is:
"I don't understand the reason or purpose of this."

"I have not worked with this partner before. Will it be okay to make a mistake with him/her?"

The students should have a clear understanding of the goal or purpose of the activity.

If possible, they should have input into the "reward." This is immediate "feedback," and monitors their accomplishment of the goal.

E.g., *"If your team follows the Ground Rules today and earns 3 tallies, your team will be successful."* The partners can "celebrate" by giving their team handshake and chant.

OR: *"If your team finishes the product/paper within the Target Time, your team will earn 1 bonus point toward..."*

The "reward" or goal for which the students are striving must **fit the needs** of the student(s).

If the teacher always choses/selects the rewards, the students might not "buy-in" to the goal/purpose.

A team which is having difficulty working successfully might need to set a measurable goal together. They should also establish a way to measure or monitor their progress.

E.g., A team that gives one another "put-downs" can concentrate on giving "encouragement." as a goal.

They could then use Encouragement Skill Cards or make tallies on their paper or Team Card to monitor how many times they gave encouragement to one another.

Each time they work together they will continue this technique to improve the number of encouraging statements until they reach their "goal."

Refer to: GOALS-REWARDS, pages 52 & 53
Refer to: SIMPLE STRUCTURES -Encourager Skill Cards, page 39

Other things to keep in mind
Seating Arrangement:
Look at your seating arrangement, are the desks side-by-side? Or are students two desks apart or across a table from one another?

If they are too far apart there is a natural breaking in the "bond" between them or work might be upside down, causing feelings of "separateness."

Shared/Limited Materials
Are the materials limited/shared? Or are the students allowed to use their individual sets of resources and move at their own pace without their partner?

Limiting materials forces partners to move in more closely, giving them the message they are doing this together.

If the seating arrangement and the materials are an issue, students experience a "barrier" between themselves and their partner.

Debriefing
In the "Wrap-up" session there should be specific questions directed to the students (written or oral) which focus on:
"How did you and your partner work together?"
"List two ways you and your partner can improve."
Refer to: Debriefing Highlights, pages 59-65

STUDENTS NOT ABLE TO COME TO AGREEMENT

We cannot *assume* students have the social skill of knowing how to reach agreement or consensus.

Some teachers assume falsely if they leave the students alone long enough, when trying to reach agreement, they will work it out by themselves.

This approach might be compared to handing a nonreader a book, leaving them alone with the book and expecting the nonreader will learn how to read!

The process of reaching agreement or consensus is a skill which needs to be **taught** in a step-by-step process. Then modeled, applied, practiced, and feedback given.

The following are five steps a teacher might use with students, or better yet, make up three or four with the class so they understand and can model them together.

A Process for Reaching Agreement/Consensus:

• Clearly explain your idea

• Give a rationale, reason for your idea.(Use the word "because").

• Listen to others' ideas and add to their ideas.

• Encourage and give praise.

• Realize your idea may not always be selected.

With younger students a teacher might want to choose three or four steps and role-play these with the students or with puppets or have students role-play parts.

Relate examples of incidents from the classroom, playground, hallways, cafeteria or from home. Using specific examples directly relating to the skill offers stronger impact.

Make cards with specific incidents on them for the teams to answer by agreeing. In teams, the students will reach consensus with their partner by going through the steps for reaching agreement.

If there is a "stubborn" teammember who will **never** give in, there is a role called: "Agreer."

Assign the Agreer role within a team to those who always have to have their way and will never give-in to others' opinions or ideas.

"Today, I am assigning you the role of Agreer. An Agreer always agrees with his/her partner."

Often the "hold out," who never agrees, has never experienced "giving-in" to another person. The Agreer role allows the student this experience in a non-threatening format.

Go to another team to observe is another technique to show those who do not have the experience or skills to reach agreement a model.

The teacher should select an "exemplary" team which will be observed. Agreer Skill Cards might be used so the Observer(s) can monitor how equally each teammember is giving feedback.

Refer to: Observer Cards, page 39
Refer to: Reaching Agreement-Consensus, page 142

TEAMS BEING TOO NOISY

Often teachers are concerned about the noise level in their classroom while teams are working together. The noise is usually projecting a productive, "on-task" atmosphere.

Yet, teachers are concerned about how their colleagues or supervisor might perceive this noise level if their colleagues do not understand the Cooperative Learning teaching strategies.

Therefore, a low noise level is important to most teachers using and adjusting to cooperative team learning.

Ideas for Lowering the Noise Level

Warning Cards dropped:
As the teacher monitors, a "warning" card (3x5 card) may be dropped on a team's table if other approaches or warnings have been issued. (Use the Warning Card as a "last resort" or major offense).

This card should state the violation:

```
WARNING!
Quiet voices
```

If the violation is not stated, the students will be questioning, *"What's this for?" "We didn't do anything!"*

After the warning card is dropped, what are the teacher's options?
The teacher will have to decide what the next step will be. Possibilities can include:

• If the behavior corrects itself the card can be picked up. (No rewarding, or the students will get the idea quickly that they can be noisy and then rewarded).

OR:
• When the behavior corrects itself, drop a new card:

```
Thank you for using:
Quiet voices
```

OR:
• Take away a tally, etc. if more than one "Warning" Card is dropped on one team table.

OR:
• Award a tally, stamp, bonus point, etc. to all teams who did not receive warning cards.

NOTE: Warning Cards can be used for any inappropriate behavior. Write the behavior on the card before it is dropped.

During the Debriefing session discuss Warning Cards. Ask the student/team for feedback on, *"How might Warning Cards be avoided?"* Or *"Discuss in your team what you will do next time to avoid a Warning Card."*

"Reteaching" Quiet Voices
Give the Signal to Stop. Get everyone's attention and reteach a quiet voice. In a soft voice say:

"In a Quiet Voice share the answer to number four..."
"This is the noise level I want you to continue using as you work with your partner."

Have a Student Noise Level Signal
The students should have a uniform **visual** signal they can use if they have difficulty hearing or know that the noise level is too high.

Students Noise Signals can include:
√ Have a red card on each team table. When it is raised, the teacher can alert the rest of the class.
√ Hand signal: Hand in the air with fingers in the "OK " circle.

√ Hand in the air waving.

√ Have the students come up with their own ideas for a Student Noise Signal.

When the signal is acknowledged, the teacher draws this to the class' attention:
"There is a noise level signal. Please lower your voices."

Red Card-Green Card
Have two-sided cards on each table. One side is red, the other side is green.

When the green side is showing there is a possibility of feedback from the teacher, (praise, tallies, stamps, bonus points, etc.).

If the teacher turns the red side up, a behavior needs correcting.

As the teacher turns the card to the red side, s/he shares softly the infraction in the affirmative:

E.g.,   "Quiet Voices"
Or: "Take Turns"
Or: "Encourage your partner"
    (If put-downs are overheard).

Note: Instead of a Red/Green card, the Team Card could be used. When it is turned over, there is an offense and no positive feedback-reward will be given when it is turned down.

SOME STUDENTS UNWILLING TO WORK IN A TEAM

How large is the team? Often, if a student is placed in a smaller team, s/he functions better. S/he learns the skills necessary to later work with others,or moves into Partner Teams of diads.

Composition of the team? Putting boy-girl combinations together often helps behavior.

Some students believe they can work better and faster by themselves. Once they realize that this is not an option when a cooperative activity is in place, they begin to adapt and appreciate the benefits of a team.

Often teachers "tire" of the complaints from students and allow them to work by themselves, This is a mistake. How can students learn the much needed social skills and the ability to accept one another in spite of differences if, in fact, they are exempt from these life, skill-building experiences?

When students complain, *"I don't want to do math!"* Do we give in and allow them not to do math?

The more practice and time a student experiences in a team format, the more comfortable s/he becomes as they acclimate themselves to the expectations and procedure.

If a student says, *"I don't want to work in a team!"* what they might actually mean is..."*I don't know how to work in a team, I don't know what is expected.*"

Help this student by allowing him/her to have the role of the Observer for a lesson or more, not being a participant. S/he can watch a team (of the teacher's choice), possibly take data or issue Skill Cards, or just observe.

Follow up by having the Observer give the teacher specific feedback of what was noticed while observing.

Once the Observer learns how other teams function, and sees how they are enjoying and benefiting from teamwrok, s/he will be ready to join a team.

When the Observer is confident, knowing the expectations and how teams function, partner him/her with someone of the opposite gender.

This technique (Observer) is appropriate for students who have not been in a cooperative learning environment.
Refer to: SIMPLE STRUCTURES-Observer, page 39

What is the reward-feedback?
Often a student does not want to do teamwork if s/he believe the reward-feedback does not meet their needs.

Evaluate your feedback-reward system and get input from the student(s).

I have had high school teachers share that they give their students stickers! The students put these on their folders/notebooks, compare them with other teams and are very proud of them.

Remember:
High school and college football coaches give their players decals to place on their helmets for a job well done!
    Goal + Reward = Feedback

COOPERATIVE LEARNING TAKES TOO MUCH TIME

NOTES:

Some teachers believe they have to put many hours and preparation into materials for cooperative learning lessons. This does NOT have to be the case.

Teach lessons as you would naturally. During the questioning session:

√ Have the students "huddle," with their partner (Partner Share) to discuss answer options and rationale.

√ Use the Simple Structure format and apply it to any lesson, E.g., *"In Round Robin format, do the questions on page ___, with your partner."*

√ Teach a lesson; have the students do the guided practice activity with their partner, using limited materials. Less correcting for the teacher!

√ Have the students write their individual stories or papers, and "team" with their partner to edit revise or compare answers, changing answers only if they can convince each other by rationale, reasoning and proof (using the word "because").

√ Review for tests in teams. Award points, tallies, stickers, bonus points,etc., if the team's average improves from the pretest; thus, encouraging teammates to help one another learn the information. Individual scores are still given for grading purposes.

Remember: Any lesson which is done individually can be adapted into a Cooperative Activity by limiting materials, taking turns, reaching agreement, teaching an idea, etc.

THE STUDENT NO ONE WANTS IN THEIR TEAM

This is a concern of most teachers - what to do with the students others shun.

This issue is addressed, and ideas are given in the section:
Structuring the Classroom, page 9

NOTES

SUPERVISING THE TEACHER USING COOPERATIVE LEARNING

Section 10

Includes:
Checklist for Teacher Observation

This section is designed for those educators who supervise, evaluate, or support teachers using Cooperative Learning Strategies.

For colleagues who peer-coach, principals and supervisors of teachers, this section covers:
- √ What to expect
- √ How to give feedback
- √ What to notice while observing

The [caution signal image] "caution" signals are in this section to remind you that often when a team does not work well, a Caution Signal should be considered, and possibly a change needs to take place. To avoid confusion and to identify the team difficulty, only one change at a time should occur.

When observing a cooperative classroom, it is important to the teacher being observed that the observer give him/her specific, constructive feedback.

Whether the teacher is being observed by a colleague in a "peer coaching" format or by a supervisor, there are things which need to be in place for constructive feedback to be helpful.

A Common Vocabulary
When Signal to Stop, Goal, Partner Share, Team Share, Debriefing, Social Skills, Ground Rules, Appreciation Statement, Round Robin, Individual Accountability, etc. are referenced, is the meaning clear to all persons involved in the observation?

What Are the Most Common Difficulties When Using Teams?
When the teacher being observed and the observer go step-by-step down the Caution Signals, can some of the difficulties being experienced with the teams be corrected?

E.g., One of the most common difficulties with teams not working well is team size, teams being too large.

By going down the checklist of "Cautions," correct one at a time. If there are still difficulties, move on to the next "Caution" Signal.

How Much Direct Instruction is Necessary in a Cooperative Lesson or Activity?
Teachers will need to cut back on their instruction-interaction and allow more time for students to Partner Share, Team Share, discuss, paraphrase, brainstorm, and to be actively involved in their lessons.

If the lesson being observed is a review activity, the teacher might be formatting the activity (directions for the activity), stating the social skill, (behavior while working together), and establishing a goal for the teams to work toward while doing the activity, (what the teams need to accomplish to be successful).

The student teams will then take over. They may be doing a Partner Share activity in a Round Robin format (taking turns) or possibly an Interview format:
E.g., One student will ask a question(s), and their partner responds. Partners switch roles, and the second partner asks questions and their partner responds.

The teacher's role is to be consistently monitoring and giving positive feedback to teams when appropriate, and giving assistance when necessary.

If the teacher has a feedback/reward system of marking Team Cards or awarding tallies, bonus points, etc., s/he should give each team **equal feedback**.

To make this section clearer, if you have not read the sections prior to this section, please do so before continuing.

NOTE: Trustbuilding-bonding is not in this section. When going into a classroom, usually the teacher will have the students in teams and functioning. Therefore, bonding will not usually be observed in this lesson. It should have occurred when forming the new teams.
Refer to: Trustbuilding-Bonding,
pages 7, 13, 14, 27-29, 68

A partner turns his/her back to partner, pulls his/her desk away, folds his/her arms, refuses to work in a team.

This symptom indicates that possibly not enough bonding has occurred for this team.

Other reasons can Include:
The reward-feedback is not meeting this student's "need" level.

Or, s/he does not understand the reason / purpose of working in teams or possibly this activity. Was the rationale explained, and did checking for understanding occur?

Or, s/he does not know or understand team expectations, and possibly needs to observe other student teams so these teams may serve as models for those who do not know the expectations.

What to expect when walking into a Cooperative Learning Classroom
Noise level: There will and should be a noise level. Students interacting, sharing ideas, opinions, and teaching one another. This is a productive, on-task noise level.

Refer to: Most Frequent Difficulties in Cooperative Learning-Teams Being Too Noisy, pages 77 & 78 -for suggestions to assist the teacher, if this is a concern of the teacher.

A Cooperative Classroom will exhibit an atmosphere of "we-ness."

Possibilities might include:
Team work displayed, Ground Rules posted visibly, Team Cards on the team desks, team logos, signs identifying teams, bulletin board display, student "vision" statements on why they enjoy being in a team, etc.

Students work more compatibly in teams when experiencing a "we" atmosphere.

ROOM ARRANGEMENT
Partners will be sitting side-by-side facing the front (teacher). No backs will be to front or the teacher and work should be right-side up.
Refer to: Structuring the Classroom -Room Arrangement, pages 11, 12, 155

TEAM SIZE
For maximum interaction, class control, and the highest level of involvement, teams of two are the ideal team size. Teams of two also boast the highest level of success.

The major reason most teams have difficulty is teams being too large.
Refer to: Structuring the Classroom - Team Size, page 6

A DIRECT INSTRUCTION LESSON
"In the typical classroom, the teacher does eighty percent of the talking."
-Goodlad

If this is correct, this leaves twenty percent interaction time for the students. In a fifty-sixty minute class period, this leaves about 20 seconds per student for interaction.

If we refer to Glasser's studies on how we learn:

70% is what we discuss with others.
80% is what we experience personally.
95% is what we teach someone else.

The teacher in a cooperative learning classroom will be reducing direct teacher instruction. S/he will allow the students to "seek" answers, share opinions with their partners, other teams and with the entire class, thereby, raising and enhancing higher level thinking, reasoning, and communicating skills.

THE TEACHER'S ROLE

The teacher will set up the lesson, (academic objective) giving the directions for the activity/task.

Next, s/he will choose, or have the teams assist in choosing, a social skill (behavior) which the lesson reinforces. Eg. Take turns, or encourage your partner, or come to agreement, etc.

S/he will not assume the students already know this skill; it will be taught, modeled by the students, and reinforced during the lesson.
Refer to: Structuring the Classroom -Social Skills, pp.14-17

A goal will be established with the students. What must the team do to be successful? (The reason or purpose of the lesson/activity is often omitted by a teacher).
Refer to: Structuring the Classroom -Goals, pages 19, 51

The teacher will tell the teams what materials are needed, if they will be limited/shared, or if each partner will work on his/her own materials or paper.

Roles will be assigned, if necessary or appropriate, to include and keep everyone involved. Keep in mind that, in small teams, involvement is built into the format by using the rule "Take Turns" or by implementing the Simple Structure -Round Robin.
Refer to: Simple Structures- Round Robin, p. 34

If roles are assigned

Are they shared so each partner is equally involved? Or, is there a reader who reads for 5 minutes, then the writer who writes one word? This is not equal involvement.

Are the roles necessary?
Explanation and direction giving for the roles is time consuming. Additional time is needed to check for understanding to be sure the teammembers all understand their roles/jobs. A teacher might need to evaluate the use of roles. If Taking Turns and/or Round Robin or other structures keep the partners involved, are roles necessary?

A target time will be established (study skill) so the students will know the time constraints, how long they have to accomplish the task. Shortly before the target time expires the teacher will announce a warning time so teams can draw closure to their task. E.g., *"You have 5 minutes remaining".*

Before the teams begin working the teacher will check for understanding of the instructions, not "Are there any questions?"
Option: *"Turn to your partner, share the directions. When you and your partner agree on the directions, thumbs up."*

For those teams who do not raise their thumbs, another team can share their directions with them.

Note: often checking for understanding is omitted in a lesson.

WHILE THE STUDENTS ARE WORKING
The Teacher's Role: Wandering, moving among the teams, <u>not</u> staying with any one team an extended period of time.

It will <u>not</u> be necessary for the teacher to reteach (except under unique circumstances) what the teacher has already taught:

If team "A" is in need of assistance, the teacher can direct them to another team for explanation. Ninety-five percent of how we learn is when we "teach" others.

MONITORING to be assured that team "A" now understands the information, the teacher can now ask them to explain it to her/him or to another team.

FEEDBACK- the teacher will be watching/listening for appropriate behavior, e.g., being on task, quiet voices, taking turns, enouraging partners, using "because" to give reason/rationale for answers.

Positive feedback will be given to teams in the form of a smile, pat on back, praise, *"good job of..."*, stamps, bonus points on the Team Card, folder, or team work, etc., thereby reinforcing and encouraging appropriate behavior.

The teacher will interact with the teams as necessary and appropriate. **Not** offering answers, but rather questioning individuals or teams on strategies, how they arrived at an answer/solution, how they are taking turns, etc.

The teacher will not intervene

If a team is having a social difficulty, the teacher will <u>not</u> solve or resolve the problem(s).

Allowing students to resolve their own conflicts is a "teaching tool" for the students experiencing the difficulty.

When the Target Time expires the teacher will give the auditory Signal to Stop. This signal should be given any time the teacher wants the attention of the class.

This signal will be followed by a long **pause**, waiting for all the **teams'** attention <u>before</u> continuing.
Refer To: Structuring The Classroom - Signal To Stop pages 14,15, 69

If the signal to stop was clear and the teacher used the pause, but some teams/class do not respond:

OPTION:
Reteach the signal, *"When you hear, 'Everyone, your attention', what should your behavior be?"*
Elicit from the students the behavior expectations.
Example:
- Finish only the sentence you are on
- Eyes on the teacher
- Everything down
- No talking

"These are all good suggestions. If you do not stop with my signal for your attention, what should I do?"

Again, eliciting from the students opinions. They set the consequence before the action. The teacher can agree with any appropriate action:

Example:
- Take away (tallies, bonus pts, etc.)
- Drop a warning card = lose a privilege
- Owe the teacher time, etc.

Refer to: Most Frequent Difficulties in Cooperative Learning - Warning Cards, pages 77 & 78

DEBRIEFING THE LESSON

The teacher will draw closure and summarize the lesson with the entire class, with individual teams, or teams can share with teams.

The lesson/activity should end with students giving one another an appreciation/affirmation statement, (alternative to put-downs).
Refer to: Debriefing Highlights, pages 60-65

 The transition between the lesson-activity and the debriefing (summary) should flow so the team behavior will remain consistent. Often the format of the debriefing is so dramatic, the students' behavior shifts with the change. Unspoken (sometimes muttered) comments include:
"This is when we have to answer those dumb questions and get our homework assignment!"

Debriefing should be an appendage of the cooperative lesson. Debriefing should be no longer that 10 minutes. The questions or format should reflect <u>directly</u> to any or several of the following:
> Lesson/activity
> Social skill(s) (behavior)
> Goal - accomplishment
> Finished product
> Roles, if assigned

If the lesson is extended and the time is limited for debriefing an Exit Question(s) can be asked and written on the board.

The students individually answer the question on their own piece of paper, and hand it to the teacher as they leave the room. This question may serve as a grade for the individual student or information for the teacher.

Other Formats

The teacher may request written responses by the team or individually.

E.g., *"List 3 things you and your partner did to reach the goal of..."*

"What was the purpose of this lesson. List one thing you learned or found helpful."

For Younger Students:

"On the top of your paper draw ☺ if you can remember what _____ is."

"If you cannot remember, draw ☹."

With **written debriefing** the most common problems are:

• Using <u>only</u> written debriefing, students do **not** "hear" feedback from their peers and/or the teacher.
If discipline problems begin occurring, check the debriefing format.

• Over-using the same debriefing form with the same questions. Students "tire" of the format, and do not take it seriously.

When written debriefing is used interchangably with oral feedback, vary the format and questions to fit the cooperative lesson/activity.

SUGGESTION for the OBSERVER

When observing a cooperative lesson use the enclosed Checklist For Teacher Observation.
Included also in the Appendix, page 139

Check, as appropriate, your observations of the lesson on the Checklist.

In the Post Observation Conference with the teacher:

Allow the teacher who was observed to share first:
"What did you like about your lesson?"

Refer back to the YES column if you noticed the same strengths; piggyback these with specific examples:

"Yes, I noticed that when____, _____ occurred." etc., adding on any other observations you noticed from the yes category.

Again, allowing the teacher to lead:
"Was there anything in your lesson you might change or do differently with the same lesson if repeated?"

If the teacher comes up with a suggestion, acknowledge it with any feedback, specific example(s) you can offer.
"I'm glad you brought that up. I noticed the same thing. When___, __occured."

Question the teacher as to what s/he might do to correct the situation. Or if it was corrected, how will it be reinforced?
"That sounds like a very workable solution. When do you think you might try it?" (Setting a timeline).

"Good, please invite me back then to check your progress."

"Is there anything else I can do to support you?"

IF the teacher has no suggestions for improvement and you have marked "NO" in some area(s) on the Checklist, refer to only one "NO" item.

NOTE: The Checklist for Teacher Observation is categorized (somewhat) in hierarchy of importance and impact.

Choose one "NO," the closest to the top of the checklist, that you believe will have the greatest impact in assisting the teacher.

Choose a skill which, if corrected, might change behavior and the success of teams.

E.g., *"I noticed you have your students in teams of 3's and 4's. Please share with me how you determined this team size?"*
The teacher shares rationale...

OBSERVER: *"I also noticed while the teams were working, that in several teams, (be specific if possible) at least one teammember appeared not to be participating."*

Give an example:
"Brian, was reading a book; Jennifer was talking to Robert; Ann was looking out the window..."

"Did you notice any of the same behavior?"

"Any ideas on how more students could become involved?"

"I read a book, Structuring the Classroom Successfully For Cooperative Team Learning, and there are some suggestions regarding team size and participation by team members."

"I would like you like to read that section and let me know your feelings about the suggestions, and if, you make any changes, let me know how they are working."

Set a timeline to check back with the teacher or schedule another observation to show support for the teacher's decision.
E.g., *"If I don't hear from you in two weeks, I will drop by and see how things are going."*

The Observer's Checklist
Until you are familiar and comfortable with Cooperative Learning strategies and have done many observations

√ Do not try to fill out the entire checklist.

√ The boxes to the first dark line of the checklist are general observation which can be done before the lesson begins.

√ The boxes to the second dark line of the ckecklist include the set-up of the lesson, direction giving, or the teaching lesson.

√ The third section is the activity itself, which the students are doing in teams.

√ The fourth section is debriefing (closure/summary).

√ The fifth or last section is "other."
The last section (on the back of the obervation form) includes: Simple Structures. Try to identify if some are used. These structures (for the most part) keep all the students actively involved.

SUGGESTION:
√ Fill in the first section prior to the lesson.

√ Mark as many boxes as possible during lesson/activity set-up.

√ Monitor, as appropriate, the third section, Lesson/Activity.

√ Check for Debriefing (summary-closure).

√ Again, do what you are comfortable handling (section wise).

√ Each cooperative lesson you observe you will notice/recognize more elements (strategies).

> Teachers need positive feedback on what was noticed plus any constructive suggestions for improvement.

Further support can be provided:
√ Run off and circulate Cooperative Learning articles to share with staff to keep them current.

√ Provide collegial observation time so teachers can learn techniques and strategies from one another.

√ Offer free time and refreshments to those who want to attend regular "coffees" to exchange ideas and offer encouragement and suggestions to others using cooperative strategies.

√ Encourage the videotaping of activites or lessons to share with peers. Edited exerpts (no longer than 5 minutes) can be shown at staff meetings.

√ At each staff meeting set aside 5-10 minutes for sharing a cooperative learning activity or success story.

√ Show time-line support. Remind teachers regularly that as with any new technique Cooperative Learning can take as long as 1-3 years until they are comfortable and the stratagies become routine.

The comments I hear most frequently, from teachers regarding their supervisor and Cooperative Learning...

"S/He does not understand it."
"S/He does not offer me feedback."
"I do not feel I am being supported."

I hope this section helps supervisors, peer coaches, and administrators in the support and evaluation of teachers using Cooperative Learning Strategies.

Cooperatively we can do together what many of us can not do alone...
Good luck! -Teresa

Checklist For Teacher Observation - Cooperative Learning

Teacher _____   Date of Observation: _____   Date for Return: _____
Grade/Subject: _____   Date of Conference: _____   Observer: _____

	observed YES	not observed NO	Observed / Comments:
Team size two			
Some threes			
Other:			
Composition -girl/boy			
Other:			
Room arrangement: side-by-side			
No backs to the teacher			
Partners			
Diads with partners			
Class environment says "we"			
Ground Rules posted			
Two-four rules			
Positive, short, concise			
Signal to Stop used			
Pause			
Students responded			
Lesson/Activity set-up (modeling, role playing) Directions clear:			
Checked for understanding			
Social Skill(s) included list skill(s)			
social skill taught **or**			
social skill reviewed			
social skill fit the lesson			
Goal stated(team success)			
Stated purpose/rationale of lesson			
Limited/shared materials			
Roles			
roles fit the lesson			
Target time given			
Energizers used students allowed to stand/move			
Activity while students are working together Students included equally			
Noise level appropriate			
Teacher wandering			
Monitoring/Adjusting as needed			
Giving feedback			
Signal to Stop used			
Pause			
Students responded			
Energizers used students allowed to stand/move			

Debriefing (summary closure done)
Oral (circle) Written

Format: (circle any used)
    Individual   With Partner   Team Share   Interview   Other:

Teacher feedback:
    Individual   Team by Team   Whole Class   Other:

Questions asked by teacher to students or teams: Write specific questions here (verbatim).

Checklist For Teacher Observation - Cooperative Learning

Check if any Simple Structures were observed, keeping everyone involved (active participation) throughout a lesson, activity, instructions or direction giving.

> **Suggestion:** Take verbatim data on the directions given by the teacher setting up these Simple Structures. Often teachers ask the students to : *"Turn to your partner,"* before they have given the students instructions on what they will be sharing with their partner.

Refer to: Simple Structures, pages 31-40

	Observed	The directions to the students, verbatim as stated by the teacher:
Partner Share		
Team Share		
Team Stand		
Red Dot / Blue dot		
Interview		
Think - Write-Share		
Round Robin		
Jigsaw		
Paraphrase		
Brainstorm		
Oral Choral		
Folded Corners		
Colored Cards		
Skill Cards		
Observer Skill Cards		
Thumbs Up/Pens Up		
Make A Date		
Bag It / Box It		
Corners/Line Up		
Other/Comments:		

LESSON PLANS

Section 11

LESSON PLANS -ELEMENTARY

LESSON PLANS -SECONDARY

LESSON PLANS -SPECIALISTS

BULLETIN BOARD IDEAS

The following pages contain lesson plans and bulletin board ideas. Most lessons are generic and adaptable to different subjects and activities. Therefore, they are non-graded and appropriate for many grade levels.

The Social Skills (Ground Rules) may also be adapted or changed as appropriate to the lesson.

Ground Rules **must** be taught and modeled **before** the actual lesson is taught. The teachers who developed these lessons have these Ground Rules already in place, and it is just a matter of **review** before the actual lesson is initiated.

With small teams, roles are <u>not</u> necesary because the rule "Take turns" covers keeping everyone involved.

The Goal...(criteria for team success).
Students often express they would like to know the <u>purpose</u>, rationale or reason for the activity.

With close monitoring from the teacher, giving **positive** and **immediate** feedback, awarding tallies, stamps, bonus points, or praise students identify with the goal and become **excited, enthusiastic, and eager** to learn!

Using variety in Debriefing techniques is a <u>key</u> to a sucessful and effective closure to the lesson.

Feedback is essential to students to let them know how well they are doing on their social as well as academic skills.

Feedback does not have to come solelyfrom the teacher, but from teammates or other teams as well. Positive feedback from a <u>peer</u> goes a long way to reinforce approp-riate behavior and raise academic achievement.

BULLETIN BOARDS

To reinforce the attitude of a cooperative classroom, the environment should exhibit this feeling as well. Bulletin boards, team pictures, teams' work, the Ground Rules on display, desks side-by-side help to reinforce the attitude and atmosphere that...this is a cooperative classroom.

ALPHABETIZING
BY Jo Ann Evans

Team size: 2 or 3   Time limit: 15-20 minutes

ACTIVITY: To alphabetize 10 vocabulary words

SOCIAL SKILLS:
- Quiet voices
- Take turns
- Mistakes are okay
- All ideas accepted
- SIGNAL TO STOP IS...bell ringing

MATERIALS:
- 1 half sheet lined paper
- 1 pencil and eraser
- 1 list of unalphabetized words

ROLES:
Reader - reads the vocabulary words
Writer - writes the words in agreed upon order
Roles switch after every two words written

GOAL:
Alphabetize the words as a team
Follow the social skills rules to receive stamps on your TEAM card

INDIVIDUAL ACCOUNTABILITY:
Each teammember is able to tell why the words are in order
Post-test held later to check these skills

DEBRIEFING:
Huddle and decide with your teammates...

- How do you know you used 12 inch voices?

- Did your team stop with the "signal" (bell ringing)?

- Do you think your team could alphabetize our class members' names tomorrow?

Teams Share...
- With another team, share your alphabetized lists, and see if you agree on the order.
- If you do NOT agree on the order, explain why/why not.

On your Team Card...
- Look at your Team Card, why did your team receive stamps today?

- If you feel your teammembers worked well today and accomplished the GOAL, (restate the goal) give yourselves a happy face on your team card.

- If your team needs to work on getting along better, put a face with a straight mouth on your Team Card.

Appreciation statement... Finish this sentence to your teammate(s)
- I liked the way you helped me...

MATH - reaching agreement
BY Sharon Thomas

Team size: 2   Time limit: 25 minutes

ACTIVITY:
Given six different types of store-bought chocolate chip cookies, the teams will independently come to an agreement as to which is the best for the money.

SOCIAL SKILLS:

- Quiet voices
- Stay with your partner
- Ask teacher ONLY if you both have questions
- Come to agreement
- SIGNAL TO STOP IS... "Class, attention."

MATERIALS:
Each team will have SIX different chocolate chip cookies
One shared check sheet
One shared pencil

ROLES: (shared)
Taster and recorder (trade after each cookie)

GOAL: (criteria for team success)
Come to team agreement (consensus) as to which brand of chocolate chip cookie is the best buy for the money.

INDIVIDUAL ACCOUNTABILITY:
Each student will be able to give the reasons why their team chose the cookie they did.

DEBRIEFING:

In your journal write...
- What did you like about working together?
- Did your team come to agreement? If not, what problems did you have?
- What could you do to work better with your partner next time?

Appreciation statement...
- Write at least one thing your partner said or did that helped your team or made you feel good. Share this with your partner.

Teacher feedback...
- These are some things I noticed while you were working together...

Lesson Plans

READING - generic
BY Sheryl Adelott

Team size: 2   Time limit: 25 minutes

ACTIVITY:
Students will read a story from the reader in paired reading and take turns, answer the questions on **ONE** comprehension sheet.

SOCIAL SKILLS:
- Listen carefully
- Take turns
- Use 12 inch voices
- SIGNAL TO STOP IS... "Stop, look and listen." (spoken by teacher)

MATERIALS:
Shared reading book
Shared comprehension sheet
Shared pencil

ROLES:

Reader - reads _?_ paragraphs, pages, or lines.
Listener / Answerer - listens carefully to be able to assist in answering comprehension questions.

Roles switch after the designated amount of reading.
Both share in answering the comprehension questions.

GOAL: (for the team to be successful)
Hand in a completed comprehension sheet
Use quiet voices

INDIVIDUAL ACCOUNTABILITY:
Teacher monitoring, randomly asking questions.
Later...administer post-test in the form of a short answer sheet completed individually by each student.

DEBRIEFING:
Thumbs up/down...
- Did you take turns as you read the story and questions?
- Did you both answer questions?
- Did you listen carefully as your partner read?
- Did you respond immediately to the SIGNAL TO STOP?

Teacher feedback...
- Here are some things I noticed...

Appreciation statement...
- Remember to thank your partner for his/her help in this lesson.

Lesson Plans

MATH - Pattern Blocks

Team size: 2   Time limit: 30-45 minutes

ACTIVITY:
Make several geometric patterns, first from wooden pattern blocks and then record the design with paper shapes.

SOCIAL SKILLS:
- Use 12 inch voices
- Agree on design
- Take turns
- Signal to stop... "Listening position, please."

MATERIALS: for each team of 2
- wooden pattern blocks
- colored paper patterns that match the blocks
- 12" X 18" black paper (1)
- glue

ROLES:
Designer- designs the pattern
Recorder- records the pattern with paper shapes, glues
Change roles after each design/pattern

GOAL:
Complete at least two geometric designs
Follow the social skill rules

INDIVIDUAL ACCOUNTABILITY:
Teacher monitoring teams, awarding "happy face" stickers to teams following the social skills

DEBRIEFING:
Huddle with your partner and share...
- What you did to earn a "happy face" sticker.
- What you did to take turns.
- What you did to agree on the pattern/design.

All Teams Standing...
- If you met the goal of making at least 2 designs.

Appreciation statement...
- Tell your partner something they did well.

Teams Share...
- Go to another team and tell the new team if your pictures are patterns or designs.
- Tell the new team at least two things you like about their pictures.

Lesson Plans

LANGUAGE ARTS-writing
BY Myra Kiekel

Team size: 2   Time limit: 25 minutes

ACTIVITY:
Write a minimum of four (4) sentences about dinosaurs, by taking turns, thinking of ideas and writing sentences, Round Robin.
Draw a team picture to illustrate the sentences.

SOCIAL SKILLS:
- Use 12 inch voices
- Take turns
- Encourage your partner
- SIGNAL TO STOP IS..."EYES" (spoken by the teacher)

MATERIALS: (per team)
1 Booklet of Dinosaur information (or sheets of information)
1 Piece of paper for sentences
1 Piece of paper for artwork
2 pens for writing - each a different color
6 crayons (3 to each student) yellow, blue, green, red, brown, purple

ROLES:
Sentences - One student looks up information. One student writes a sentence dictated to him/her. Roles are reversed for next sentence.

Drawing - students decide on a picture to illustrate their sentences and draw and color it together, one student using only red, yellow, blue and the other using only green, brown and purple.

GOAL: (criteria for team success)
Write 4 sentences and have one team picture.

INDIVIDUAL ACCOUNTABILITY:
Teacher checks sentence writing by alternate use of pen colors.
Check picture by use of designated color usage.

DEBRIEFING:
Thumbs up/down - "Did you and your partner..."
- Use 12 inch voices?
- Stop and LOOK immediately with the signal "EYES?"
- Encourage each other?

Share outloud, by raising hands...
- What did your partner say to encourage you?

Checking GOAL...
- Stand up if your team met the goal of writing 4 sentences and drawing a team picture.

Appreciation statement...
- Give your team handshake (applause, pat, etc.,) to your partner for accomplishing your team GOAL!

Teams Share...(time permitting)
- Turn to another team and share one sentence and your team picture.
- Share something positive to the other team about their sentence and picture.

MATH - review facts
By Georgia Wells (adapted)

Team size: 2   Time limit: 20 minutes

ACTIVITY:
To review basic math facts.
Each teammember has a set of math fact cards, identical to partner's cards *(these can be run on sheets of paper, a different color for each partner, and the teammembers cut them apart to make cards)*. On one side is a math fact, on the opposite side is the fact and the answer.

Partners face each other.
> The CHECKER holds up a math fact, (the answer facing the CHECKER).
> The MATH WORKER reads the fact outloud and gives the answer.
> The CHECKER gives **praise** if the answer is correct and hands the card to the WORKER.

If the answer is incorrect the CHECKER gives **encouragement** and returns the card to the pile to be reviewed.

Roles are switched after each turn, each partner trying to earn back his/her entire set of cards.
refer to: SIMPLE STRUCTURES - Colored Cards

SOCIAL SKILLS:
- Quiet voices
- Take turns
- Mistakes are okay
- SIGNAL TO STOP IS... "May I have your attention please..."

ROLES:
Math Worker - reads the math fact and gives the answer.
Checker - looks at the answer side of the card and shares with the *Math Worker*.
If the worker's answer is correct and gives **praise /encouragement**.
ROLES are *switched* after each math fact.

MATERIALS:
- Two sets of cards with math facts to be studied on one side, on the reverse side are the facts plus the answer.
- One Team Card per team (3X5) index card with teammembers' name or team name.

GOAL: (what a team does to be successful)
- Improve your TEAM timed test score, given after this activity.
- Earn at least two stamps on your Team Card, for giving **praise** or **encouragement** to your partner.

INDIVIDUAL ACCOUNTABILITY:
The teacher will randomly check individuals for accuracy and give a timed drill at the end of the work session.
Test taken individually, scores recorded individually, then added to partner's score for TEAM IMPROVEMENT points, recognition, etc.

DEBRIEFING:
Thumbs up/down if...
- You and your partner took turns.
- You and your partner earned back at least (10, or any number) cards altogether.
- If your team received at least 2 stamps on your Team Card for giving praise.

Random check...
- Share with your partner what he/she said to encourage you.
- What is 7+8? (any math facts to check individual accountability).

Huddle with your partner and share...
- What you will do next time to help one another learn these facts?
- What you liked about how you and your partner worked together today.

PROBLEM SOLVING - mixed grade levels
BY   Joy Dutson

Team size: 2 (1 kindergartener with 1 third grader or **any grade combinations**)
teamed with another partner team of kindergarten-third grade combination
Time limit: 20-30 minutes

TRUSTBUILDING:
Sitting in diads, talk about their pets, favorite toys, games etc. (2-4minutes).

ACTIVITY:
Each team of kindergarten-third graders will present a social problem to the other team in their diad to solve. Problems are to be something that might happen either in the classroom or on the playground.
To start the process, each third-grader is given a short, simple problem on a card, they read it to the other kindergartener-third grade team to solve and then the teams make up problems-solutions from there.

Examples of starter questions could be: *There are 4 kids blocking the top of the slide. How can I get my turn? Someone tells you to "go away" when you want to join. What can you do? I need the red pen right now and it's being used. I'm in a hurry, what can I do? Tom just kicked down our block structure!   It's circle time and someone is already sitting next to my best friend...*

SOCIAL SKILLS:
- Take turns -presenting and solving
- Speak clearly so everyone understands
- Use quiet voices
- SIGNAL TO STOP IS... bell ringing

MATERIALS: Initial PROBLEM-SOLUTION card

ROLES:
Presentors one team of K& 3
Solvers second team of K& 3
Switch roles after each problem is solved

GOAL: Come up with at least **one** way to solve the problem which is presented.

INDIVIDUAL ACCOUNTABILITY:
Teacher randomly checking, monitoring,and asking directed questions during debriefing.

DEBRIEFING:
Thumbs up/down.. with your teammate...
- Did everyone on your team participate?
- Were you able to come up with at least **one** solution?
- Did everyone on your team listen?
- Would you like to do this activity again?

Randomly calling on teams...
- Third grader share one problem... Kindergartener, share the solution.
- Share with your team what you could do to improve the way you worked together...(have some teams share this).

Kindergarteners...
- Tell your partner one thing you liked about how they helped you today...

MATH - Zero the Hero
Numeral writing activity   by Debra Emerson

Team size: 2   Time limit 25 minutes

ACTIVITY: Students will fill in a grid with numbers 1-100 (or skip counting by 2's, 3's, 5's, 10's, etc).

SOCIAL SKILLS:
- Quiet voices
- Take turns
- Ask the teacher ONLY if both students have the same question

- SIGNAL TO STOP IS... ringing the bell

MATERIALS:
Worksheet containing number grid or 1" grid paper
2 crayons (different colors) per team

ROLES:
1 child reads the numerals
1 child writes the numerals
roles switch after each completed row
roles are modeled with teacher and a student before the activity begins

GOAL: (for team to be successful)
Each team will complete the number grid to 50 or more in the time limit given

INDIVIDUAL ACCOUNTABILITY:
Each child in the team writes with a different colored crayon and random checking of individuals by teacher.

DEBRIEFING: *quick*

Thumbs up if...
- you and your partner helped each other.
- you and your partner used quiet voices.
- you and your partner took turns.

Teacher: "This is what I noticed while you were working..."
- Turn to your partner and share how well you worked together (appreciation statement).

SPELLING
Colored Cards format
BY   Linda Cohoon

Team size: 2   Time limit : 10 minutes

ACTIVITY:

To practice spelling words. Students will "earn" a spelling word from their partner by correctly spelling the word aloud to a partner.

Spelling words are runoff on two colors of paper, each word in a 2 X.2.5 inch rectangle. Each teammember cuts the words out in flashcard fashion, and each teammember has a different color from his/her partner.

Partners **trade** colored cards, in order for partner to regain the original cards, the word asked by the partner must be spelled correctly. If the word is missed the card goes to the bottom of the pile.

Partners **take turns** "drilling" one another on the words within the time limit, giving suggestions and techniques which may assist the teammate in learning the words.

refer to: **SIMPLE STRUCTURES - Colored Cards**
Note: This format can be used with any subject matter for variety in review.

SOCIAL SKILLS:
- Use 12 inch voices
- Stay on the job
- Mistakes are okay
- SIGNAL TO STOP IS...bell ringing

MATERIALS:
1 set of spelling words, on cards, per teammember (a different color from partner)

ROLES:
Checker- checks the spelling of partner's oral spelling of words
Switch role after every word

GOAL:
Each teammember earns 7 out of 10 of his/her spelling words back from a partner. A sticker will be awarded to those teams who attain the goal.

INDIVIDUAL ACCOUNTABILITY: (choose one or more)
- Teacher will randomly check individuals.
- Partners go to new teams and earn their spelling words from a new partner.
- Test at end of the week.

DEBRIEFING:

Random calling of teams to find out how many words they earned back

Team Share: Teammates go to new teams and share the words they missed and have a *new* teammember "drill" them on the words to "reearn" them from a "new" team-member (possibly acquiring a *different* technique for learning the words).

Thumbs up or down...
- Did you use a 12 inch voice?
- Did you and your partner stay on the job?

Huddle and decide together...
- How did you encourage/help your partner?
- What did you say/do if your partner missed a word?

Appreciation statement...
- Share a positive statement with your partner on how well you worked together...

Lesson Plans

MATH - classifying / sorting
BY Karen Lawrence (adapted)

Team size: 2   Time limit: 15-25 minutes

ACTIVITY:

The teams will be able to sort "junk" (<u>Math Their Way</u>, boxes of assorted button, keys, bottle caps, etc.) into 2 groups by various attributes of their choice. E.g.,. size, color, texture, etc.

The teams will do at least 2 sortings in 10 minutes. (Give 2 minute target time quides)

SOCIAL SKILLS:
- Use quiet voices
- Use partner's name
- Everyone helps (everyone has junk to sort and agree)
- SIGNAL TO STOP IS...bell ringing

MATERIALS:

1 junk box per team
1 tally card (for marking when names are said)
1 pencil for marking tallies
1 piece or 18"-24" string or yarn
(formed into circle for sorting to be done inside the boundaries)

ROLES:

Recorder- tallies every time a teammember's name is used
Sorter(s) - does the activity
Switch roles after 2 minutes (2 minute target times given by teacher).

GOAL:

Receive at least 4 tallies for using one another's names
And / or earn 1 unifix cube for sharing how the sorting was done

INDIVIDUAL ACCOUNTABILITY:

Teacher will monitor teams, **randomly check** with individuals to share how the junk was sorted. (Awarding unifix cubes if teammember can explain).
TEAM SHARE: Teams will go to another team and they will share how they sorted their junk.

DEBRIEFING:

With individual teams...to earn a unifix cube
- Name one way your junk is sorted. (asking individual).
- If you are unsure, have your partner(s) explain again.

Class debriefing...
- How many teams earned at least 1 unifix cube (goal).
- Congratulate your teammate(s) by thanking them for their help (appreciation statement).
- What was your favorite way of sorting?
- How many times did your teammate(s) use names (shown by number of fingers raised)   Teacher: *"Wow, good job, you really know how to use your teammate's name! etc."*
- What could you have done to use names more? (Not pointing, not saying "Hey, you.." etc.).

READING - generic
BY Donna Medema

Team size: 2   Time limit: 20 minutes

ACTIVITY:
Students will read sentences aloud to each other sounding out words with CVC combinations (or any criteria set by teacher).

Students with mark the sentence they read with a colored X by the sentence (each student using a different colored crayon).

SOCIAL SKILLS:
- 12 inch voices
- Mistakes are okay
- Take turns
- SIGNAL TO STOP IS..."Boys and girls, may I have your attention please."

MATERIALS:
I reading sheet
2 different colored crayons

ROLES:
Reader - reads the sentence
Praiser - gives praise to reader and assists if necessary
Switch roles after each sentence

GOAL:
Teammembers will use **12 inch voices**, **take turns** reading sentences and the **praiser** will make one **positive comment** to partner. Try to get 3 stamps on team paper.

INDIVIDUAL ACCOUNTABILITY:
Teacher will monitor the children in their teams and stamp the papers of those teams on task, following the social skill rules.

DEBRIEFING:

Thumbs up/down...
- Did you use 12 inch voices?
- Did your partner praise you after you read?
- What positive comment did your partner share?
- If you had difficultly, how did your partner help?

Appreciation statement...
- Finish this sentence to your partner..."I liked the way you..."

Lesson Plans

SOCIAL STUDIES - generic
BY Lynda Wittren

Team size: 2   Time limit: 40 minutes

ACTIVITY:
To review what a port community (or any community or topic), is by *listing* things one would see (have, do, etc.) in a port community and *draw* a picture from the list.

Both teammembers are responsible for the picture, both must *sign* it and give it a *name*.

SOCIAL SKILLS:
- Quiet voices
- Stay with your team
- Take turns
- Mistakes are okay
- SIGNAL TO STOP IS: teacher claps 3 times, student repeat clap

MATERIALS:
1 Social Studies book   1 pencil
1 piece of lined paper   1 large piece of drawing paper

ROLES:
Recorder- write the list that both of you decide on
Materials handler- gathers "materials" items listed on board
Take turns drawing and planning

GOAL:
Earn four (4) tallies IIII, on team card for following the social skill rules and finish the product

INDIVIDUAL ACCOUNTABILITY:
While teams are working, teacher will award each team a tally on their team card (at their station), next to the listed social skill, goal being met.

Each team will be awarded a sticker for their team banner if they earn four tallies.

If ALL teams earn a sticker, 10 minutes free time will be awarded the class.

DEBRIEFING: questions on the board to be gone over if team finishes early

Talk it over with your partner...
- How did you and your partner take turns?
- How do you know you used quiet voices?
- Did you reach the GOAL of receiving four tallies?
- What made it possible to reach your goal?
- How did you encourage your partner?

Appreciation statement...
- Think of one positive thing your partner did to help the team reach the GOAL and thank your partner for it.

Teams Share...(time permitting)
- Go to another team and share your picture, and each partner explains one idea.

"SICK" TALLY SHEET

Team names:

POETRY - Writing
BY Kay Fawver

Team size: 2   Time limit: 40 minutes

ACTIVITY:
The teams will write a poem and make an illustration, using "SICK" as a pattern developing their skills of rhyming using couplets. (Brainstorming some rhyming "families" before teamwork begins.

SOCIAL SKILLS:
- 12 inch voices
- Take turns
- Mistakes are okay
- Encourage your partner
- SIGNAL TO STOP IS...teacher claps, students repeat clap and respond with the word "poetry!"

MATERIALS:
1 Piece of paper for writing "SICK" poem and illustration
1 Pencil
Markers for making illustration

ROLES:
None needed. Writer changes after 5 minutes, teacher giving "Target time."

GOAL:
Finish the couplet with an illustration.
Earn 5 tallies on team Tally Card (which has a "sick" picture on it!) for following the social skills as monitored by the teacher.

INDIVIDUAL ACCOUNTABILITY:
Teacher monitors and randomly checks individual's knowledge of couplets.
Writing a two line appreciation statement to their partner in a couplet.
Example: When working with YOU,
We got along well TOO!

DEBRIEFING:
Orally with the teacher...
- Did you meet the GOAL of finishing the "Sick" poem with illustration?
- What we learned today relates to only one type of poetry...the couplet.

Huddle with your partner and think of another type of Poetry.
Team Stand when you have thought of another one.

Teams Share...
- With your partner, share your couplet and illustration with another team.
Appreciation statement - Individual accountability...
- Write a two line couplet to your partner, in appreciation for the good job you did together today, an example could be ..., Now think of your own!

MATH - Story Problems
By Kathy Garling

Team size: 2   Time limit: 45 minutes

ACTIVITY:
Teams will write two story problems for multiplication, division, addition and subtraction.

Use **word clues** to determine which operation to use.

   Example: Addition-*altogether,* Subtraction -*left ,* etc. (circle these)
   Teams will then share two story problems with another team (Team Share) to solve.

SOCIAL SKILLS:
   - Quiet voices
   - Listen carefully to ideas
   - Take turns
 - SIGNAL TO STOP IS:...ringing bell

MATERIALS:
   1 piece of paper
   1 pencil

ROLES:
   Recorder - writes the story problem
   Questioner - asks questions and gives input
Roles switch after each problem

GOAL:
   Each team must finish ONE story problem for each operation and have at least ONE word clue circled for each story problem.

INDIVIDUAL ACCOUNTABILITY:
   Teacher will monitor and randomly check individuals.
   During debriefing teacher will randomly check through individual questioning of the students.

DEBRIEFING:
   Teams Share...
      - Choose two story problems to share with another team to solve.

   Predetermined questions written on blackboard...
      - Strategies we used to accomplish the activity (task) were...
      - My / Our favorite story problem is...
      - Some problems we had with the task were... What we can do differently next time is to...
      - Give your partner your secret handshake if you met the goal of...
      - What did your partner do well? Tell this to your partner.

WORD SEARCH - generic
BY Carol Olson (adapted)
Team size: 2   Time limit: 30 minutes

ACTIVITY:

Make a word search of your (spelling words, vocabulary words, social studies, math concepts, etc.

Put each word from your list, one letter per square, onto graph paper. Words may be written horizontally, vertically, diagonally, forwards or backwards. Then hide the words by filling in the remaining squares with other letters.

SOCIAL SKILLS: (rules)
- Quiet voices
- Take turns
- Use encouragement
- SIGNAL TO STOP IS:.."May I have your attention please?"

MATERIALS:
1 - 1/2 sheet of centimeter graph paper (or 1/4 sheet for fewer words)
2 - pencils or pens of different colors
1 list of words (or directions as to where the words may be found)

ROLES: Shared, by rule *Taking Turns*
Instructions to teams: be sure you and your partner both participate equally. Decide how you will work with the list, dividing it, working with one word at a time, etc. The color of ink will show me how well you took turns.

GOAL:
To receive 3 tallies on your Team Card from the teacher for following the Ground Rules and finishing the product.

INDIVIDUAL ACCOUNTABILITY:
Different colored ink, each teammember signs product with color being used.
Teacher monitoring and randomly checking individuals.

DEBRIEFING:
Thumbs up if...
- you and your partner had equal or nearly equal participation with contributing and writing. How do you know this?
- your team used quiet voices most of the time?
- your partner said/did something encouraging?
  (Call on volunteers to share what was said/done).

Teams stand if...
- you received at least 5 tallies on your Team Card for appropriate behavior.
- you met the goal of finishing the product.
Because you met the goal... give your partner your team handshake (chant, rap or whatever is appropriate).
Appreciation statement...
- as you put your things away share something positive with your partner about how well you worked together today.
For next session (or if time allows):
Teams Share...
- With another team share the word search to "find" the words, again using the colored pens. Sign your name in the color you are using.

SOCIAL STUDIES - generic
BY Carol Crockett

Team size: 2   Time limit: 20 minutes

ACTIVITY:
Learn one explorer in the Western Hemisphere (or any topic of study).
Each team looks up 1 explorer drawn randomly from prepared names on cards. Information to be included: For which country they explored, date, area explored.
(At a later class time, all 12 explorers, dates, countries, etc. will be distributed on cards for teams to study and review).

SOCIAL SKILLS: (Classroom poster displays these Ground Rules).
- 12 inch voices
- Stay on task
- One person talks at a time
- Positive praising (put-downs not allowed)
- SIGNAL TO STOP IS:... "Listen up"

MATERIALS:
Card with name of explorer
1 pencil
1 reference book

ROLES:
Reader -reads information
Recorder- writes down information agreed upon
Roles switch after each question

GOAL:
Earn 5 tallies on team card for following the Ground Rules (social skills).
By the end of five activity days know all 12 explorers.

INDIVIDUAL ACCOUNTABILITY:
TEST after five activity days.

DEBRIEFING:
Referring to the "Ground Rules" chart posted..."Huddle and..."
- Think of two things that went well and why...
- What is one thing you could have done differently and how would you improve it ?
- What did you say/do to encourage your partner?

Teacher feedback...
- These are some things I noticed...
Appreciation statements...Choose one to finish from sentence strips...
- "I felt good when..."
- "___, you really helped me when..."

REPORT (BOOK) -generic
BY John Otto

Team size: 2   Time limit: 30 minutes

ACTIVITY:
Evaluate (critique) a book (or **any other material or report**) and prepare to present the results, (in Team Interview format), to another team by following the Book Review Form.

SOCIAL SKILLS: (ground rules)
- 12 inch voices
- Use encouragement
- Take turns
- Mistakes are okay
- SIGNAL TO STOP IS:... "May I have your attention!"

MATERIALS:
1 Book Review Form (on next page)
1 paper for writing critique
2 pencils/ pens -different color ink/lead

ROLES:
Reader - reads the Book Review Form
Scribe - writes down the evaluation notes
Rotate these roles

GOAL:
Follow the ground rules, earn three tallies on Team Card
Finish the product, critique a book

INDIVIDUAL ACCOUNTABILITY:
Colored ink to show involvement.
Teacher monitoring, randomly checking individuals for input.
Team Interview, paraphrasing what they learned / heard.

DEBRIEFING:

Team Interview...When partnering with another team...
- Be prepared to ask another team who, what, why, when, etc. questions about their book and the report itself.

- Be prepared to "share" with another team the main idea, characters, plot and other information.

- Be sure to give your partner team positive feedback.

- Share with your partner two things you did well because you worked together.

BOOK REVIEW FORM

TITLE

I First paragraph - Introduction
Title and author
Setting: time and place
Main characters: a *brief* description
Fiction or nonfiction

II Next paragraph(s): Main events of the plot
Brief summary of the *plot*
Choose two or three *important events* and describe
briefly. (For a nonfiction book choose interesting or
important facts or ideas

III Last paragraph - conclusion
Evaluation: What did you think of the book and why?
Fast or slow paced
Easy or difficult to read
High or low interest level
Believable characters - do the characters seem real?
Recommendation: do you recommend this book to others?
Why or why not?

SPEECH EVALUATION

NAME _____   DATE _____

TOPIC _____   GRADE _____

INTRODUCTION	1 2 3 4 5 6 7 8 9 10
APPEARED CALM AND POISED	1 2 3 4 5 6 7 8 9 10
POSTURE	1 2 3 4 5 6 7 8 9 10
GRAMMAR AND WORDING	1 2 3 4 5 6 7 8 9 10
VOICE PROJECTION	1 2 3 4 5 6 7 8 9 10
EYE CONTACT	1 2 3 4 5 6 7 8 9 10
USE OF VISUAL AIDS	1 2 3 4 5 6 7 8 9 10
STATED IDEAS CLEARLY	1 2 3 4 5 6 7 8 9 10
REMAINED WITHIN THE TIME LIMIT	1 2 3 4 5 6 7 8 9 10
CONCLUSION	1 2 3 4 5 6 7 8 9 10

total points _____

SPEECH
cooperative evaluation
BY   Cheryl Gramson

Team size: 2   Time limit: speech 2-5 min.
                                Team evaluation 2 min.

ACTIVITY:
As the speaker is giving the speech, each teammember will complete a speech evaluation sheet.

After the speech, using these sheets, the **team** will **write** at least three, **positive and constructive** comments to include: *"The two best things about this speech were..."* AND *"One thing the speaker could do to improve his/her speech is..."*

The teacher will call on several teams randomly to give their, agreed upon, comments.

SOCIAL SKILLS: (Ground Rules)
- Quiet voices
- Take turns - sharing ideas
- Come to agreement
- SIGNAL TO STOP IS:.."May I have your attention!"

MATERIALS:
2 Speech Evaluation sheets (preceeding page)
2 pencils
1 paper for writing positive/constructive comments

ROLES: (for the positive/constructive commentary only)
Reader- reads the scores from the speech evaluations
Writer - writes the comments (based on discussion of data from speech evaluations) on the comment sheet
GOAL:
To reach agreement on the commentary sheet
Follow the Ground Rules and earn stamps on Team Card

INDIVIDUAL ACCOUNTABILITY:
Each member will complete a Speech Evaluation Sheet.

DEBRIEFING:
Huddle with your partner and discuss...
- What are the strenghs of this format of evaluation? Weaknesses?
- What kinds of comments were the most helpful?
- Was it difficult to reach agreement on the comments? Why / Why not?

Team Stand if...
- Your team received at least 4 stamps on your Team Card.
- Now share with your partner, why you received 2 of your stamps.

Appreciation statement...
- Write one thing your partner did to help your team reach its goal, share this with your partner.

Lesson Plans

ENGLISH - Parts of Speech
BY Merilyn Dunn (adapted)

Team size: 2   **Time limit: 20-30 minutes**

ACTIVITY:

The teams will be able to recognize and group word cards under the headings NOUN - VERBS - ADJECTIVES **(or use any topic/subject as a substitute).**
They will then write the word, from the card under the correct heading on the sheet of paper which has the headings.

SOCIAL SKILLS:

- Quiet voices
- Take turns
- Mistakes are okay   (review what they can say to one another if they make a mistake)
- Encouraging - no "put downs"
- SIGNAL TO STOP IS..."Stop - Look at me - Listen."

MATERIALS:

Word cards for each team
1 Pencil
1 Large piece of paper with headings: VERB - NOUN - ADJECTIVE

ROLES:

Using role cards-

Recorder - writes the word when the person with the card tells where it is to go. Each person takes turns with a Word Card, telling if it should be written under the N - V - ADJ heading.

Checker - asks the partner where s/he thinks the word goes and asks them why they think it goes there.

"What do you think?" Why do you think it goes there?" can be written on the role cards to be used as a "script" for the **checker**.

Change roles after 3 cards - exchange role cards-

GOAL:

To place all the word cards under categories with mutual agreement.
Teacher gives tallies for following social skills, teams work for 4 tallies.

INDIVIDUAL ACCOUNTABILITY:

Teammembers sign the product. Do a worksheet independently, check answers with partner after completed.

DEBRIEFING:

- What is one word your team put under the __?__ heading (N - V - ADJ.)?

- Were the word cards too easy / difficult?

- What went well in your team?

- What might you do to make this activity easier?

- How did your team earn a tally point?

- Did you and your partner take turns?

- Did your team meet the goal of putting all the word cards under the headings?

- Complete this statement to your partner, using their name..."___, you did a good job of ..."

Lesson Plans

MATH - Digit Draw - generic
By Charlista Barttels
Team size: 2   Time limit: 40 minutes

ACTIVITY:
Students will compose multiplication (addition, subtraction, division, fractions, money, etc. can be used as an option),and solve them.

The **"Card Drawer,"** randomly draws numeral cards and set them up to make a multiplication problem according to the format on the record sheet.

The **"Solver,"** then records the solution to the problem as the team determines answers. S/he then uses the calculator to check the team answer. They continue using the Round Robin format doing as many problems as time permits.
Example of one question from the record sheet format: students fill in with the randomly drawn numerals.

SOCIAL SKILLS:
- Quiet Voices
- Take Turns
- Encourage Your Partner
- Mistakes Are Okay
- Signal to Stop is... *"Please be ready to listen."*

MATERIALS: one set per team

1 set numeral cards 1-9
1 record sheet and pencil
1 calculator

ROLES:
Card Drawer - draws numeral cards, sets up the problem according to the format on the record sheet and records it.

Solver - records the solution on the record sheet and checks the answer with the calculator.

Roles are exchanged after each problem.

GOAL:
Each team will try to accomplish one or both goals:
Using the team will try to set up at least and solve at least 10 problems (whatever number is reasonable and that **most** teams can accomplish), in the Target Time given, (30 minutes or whatever time is appropriate).

They will try to receive at least two tallies (stamps, bonus points, etc.) from the teacher, feedback indicating they are staying on task and encouraging their partner.

INDIVIDUAL ACCOUNTABILITY:
Teacher monitoring as the teams are working. Worksheets will be handed in.
An Exit Quiz (two to four problems done individually), or a test can be administered.

DEBRIEFING:
Written- On the back of your team worksheet, take turns writing a response.
- We took turns by...
- If we had difficulty we...
- One thing we did well was to...
- One thing we can improve on is...
- My partner helped me by...
(Be sure to use each partner's name and write something about each).
© C&M EDUCATION CONSULTANTS

115

WRITING - Editing (Interview format)
BY Dawn Corliss (adapted)

Team size: 2 (Team Share in 4)   Time limit: 20-30 minutes

ACTIVITY:
Individuals will have independently written an article for the classroom newspaper. Teams of 2 will Team Share in diads (4) to edit and revise each other's articles.

SOCIAL SKILLS:
- 12 inch voices
- Stay on task
- Mistakes are okay
- Use encouragement (have students share encouraging statements)
- SIGNAL TO STOP IS: ringing of bell

MATERIALS:
Paper to write article
4 Different colored marking pens (1 per person)

ROLES:
Person **A** and person **B** will proofread each other's articles.
Person **C** and person **D** will do the same.

Person **A** will then explain to the other three the changes s/he made and why.
Each of the other three will do the same, in turn.

While the three are listening, they may be noting other revisions and make further corrections with their individual colored pen.

GOAL:
Each member must contribute something to the proofreading - revision process. Every team having all four colors and matching initials (students sign in their pen color), showing proofreading symbols and revisions, will receive... (reward- bonus points, free time, etc.)

INDIVIDUAL ACCOUNTABILITY:
The teacher will be able to identify initials and colors on proofread/revised papers. S/he will be able to observe this in progress as s/he monitors as well as checking the finished product.

DEBRIEFING:
Orally with teacher...

- Raise your hand if your team has completed the assigned task.

- Huddle together and talk over what you learned from your teammates today.

- Huddle and share what you said to one another that was encouraging.

- Discuss with your team the most common errors made by all of you, be prepared to share your team ideas with the class.

- How many teams met the GOAL? GREAT! Your team has earned...

- Share with your teammates, *"We did a good job of..."*

MATH - fractions
BY Lois McGlothin (adapted)
Recipe by Susan Mobley
Team size: 2   Time limit: 30-45 minutes

ACTIVITY: In teams reduce the fractions in the given recipe down to lowest terms.

COOKIE RECIPE

Preheat oven to 375°   Stir together:

$\frac{12}{24}$ c. flour = _____

$\frac{45}{90}$ tsp baking powder = _____

$\frac{25}{100}$ tsp salt = _____

$\frac{3}{12}$ tsp cinnamon = _____

$\frac{9}{36}$ tsp ginger = _____

ADD:
$\frac{51}{102}$ c. brown sugar = _____

$\frac{18}{36}$ c. rolled oats = _____

$\frac{2}{16}$ c. oil = _____

$\frac{7}{7}$ egg = _____

$\frac{36}{24}$ c. raisins = _____

$\frac{12}{4}$ tsp milk = _____

When completely blended, drop by teaspoons onto greased cookie sheet.   Bake 8-12 minutes.

Variations $\frac{3}{3}$ c. chocolate chips = _____ or $\frac{13}{13}$ c. peanut butter = _____

substitute $\frac{4}{4}$ tsp vanilla = _____ in place of ginger and omit cinnamon.

SOCIAL SKILLS: (Ground Rules)
- Quiet voices
- Take turns
- Mistakes are okay
- Encourage your partner
- SIGNAL TO STOP IS...bell ringing

MATERIALS: Cookie recipe- to be reduced
2 pencils/pens different colors of ink/lead

ROLES: Partner Share-
Reader - reads the fraction, solves the problem with input from partner
Recorder - records the answer
Roles switch after each problem

GOAL:
To follow the Ground Rules, and earn Tallies on Team Card
Arrive at correct answers for at least 8 of the fractions

INDIVIDUAL ACCOUNTABILITY:
Colored ink/lead shows degree of involvement
Teacher monitoring and random checking of individuals

DEBRIEFING:
Teams Share...
- With your partner, go to another team and compare answers, be able to defend your answer unless convinced otherwise. Go to three different teams and do the same.

Written evaluation...
- On the bottom of your team recipe write: What your team did well, if you met the goal (if not, why), what you learned by going to others teams to share, one positive thing each of you contributed to the team activity.

© C&M EDUCATION CONSULTANTS

FOREIGN LANGUAGE-generic
BY Linda Kreis (adapted)
Team size: 2   Time limit: 30-45 minutes

ACTIVITY:
To correctly and fluently respond to questions in **foreign language** readings. This will be done individually, partners will Partner Share their answers and come to consensus on answers.

Practice these questions in Partner Share to be prepared for an oral quiz at a later date. (Teammember asks question in **foreign language** and partner responds in same language).

SOCIAL SKILLS: (Ground Rules)
- Quiet voices
- Encourage your partner
- Take turns
- Mistakes are okay
- SIGNAL TO STOP IS: "May I have your attention please!" (in foreign language)

MATERIALS:
1 set of questions - divided between teammembers
1 pen/pencil per student (different colors)
1 team paper with one set of answers

ROLES:
none - Taking Turns covers this-

GOAL:
By following the Ground Rules teams will be awarded "foreign currency" (funny money) during their work/review time which can be traded for a ("free assignment," free time, or whatever the teacher and class decide as appropriate).

INDIVIDUAL ACCOUNTABILITY:
Doing several questions individually, different colored ink.
Teacher monitoring, checking randomly for accuracy.

DEBRIEFING:
Teams Share...
- With another team, - **Team A** asks a question in a foreign language **Team B** responds. (teammembers take turns asking and responding, but can consult with partner for assistance).

Huddle with your teammate...
- How many "Pesos" (any foreign currency) did your team earn and why?

Team huddle and write...
- What was difficult about this assignment? What can your team do differently?
- What were the benefits of practicing with another team?
- If you were to change this activity, what would you do differently?

- Write two things your team did well during this activity.
- On a scale of 1-5, with 1 being ,NOT READY and 5 being VERY READY, rate your team on how prepared you are for the oral quiz.

Appreciation statement...
- Share with your partner something positive on how they assisted you today.

BAND
BY Matthew Harden
Team size: 3   Time limit: 20 minutes

ACTIVITY:
Students will learn to work with various rhythm patterns by completing the worksheet on rhythm, in teams, and counting out the exercises.

SOCIAL SKILLS: (Ground Rules)
- Pianissimo voices (pp=very soft)
- Take turns
- Listen carefully to others
- Mistakes are okay
- SIGNAL TO STOP IS: **do, mi, so** - played by teacher

MATERIALS:
1 worksheet of rhythms
1 pencil

ROLES:
Recorder - *records* what the team agrees upon, notes, counting numerals and signs; gets all teammembers' signature on worksheet.
Encourager - gives *positive feedback* to teammembers about their contributions by telling them how helpful they are.
Rhythm expert - *checks* to make sure that rhythms are written correctly, that measures have the right number of counts and that counting is written correctly.

GOAL: (criteria for success)
Teams must complete the worksheet, OR at least 14 of 20 items.
ALL teams completing the worksheet will be allowed to choose their favorite piece to rehearse on Friday.

INDIVIDUAL ACCOUNTABILITY:
Teacher monitoring, random checking on individuals for feedback.
Post-test given individually, at later date, similar to worksheet.

DEBRIEFING:
Huddle with your team and decide...
- How did the Rhythm Expert help you check your answers?
- How did you take turns? What 2 ways could your team improve on taking turns?
- What did the Encourager say or do to help you feel successful?
- If you were the teacher what would you do to help your students feel more successful?

Teacher feedback...
- These are some things I noticed...

Appreciation statement...
- Give eye contact to your teammembers and individually share a positive statement about their performance in the team today. (Ask for volunteers to share some statements)

119

HOME ECONOMICS
BY   Carole Boersma

Team size: 2 or 3   Time limit: 25 minutes

ACTIVITY:
Using pictures from a magazine, make a collage of **at least** five foods your team can agree upon as being "good to eat."

Lead-in activity for discussion about food likes and dislikes.

SOCIAL SKILLS: (Ground Rules)
- Quiet voices
- Take turns
- Use encouragement
- Come to agreement
- SIGNAL TO STOP IS: bell ringing - followed by, "heads up!"

MATERIALS:
1 magazine	1 piece -construction paper
1 pr. scissors	1 pencil
1 bottle glue	

ROLES:
Researcher - *has magazine and pencil* - **looks** through the magizine for a picture and calls out the name of the food pictures until all agree on a food to be included in the collage. S/he initials the picture after it is pasted.

Cutter - *has scissors* - **cuts** out the picture.

Paster - *has glue bottle* - **arranges** and **glues** the picture on the paper.

Roles are rotated after each picture selection

GOAL: (criteria for team success)
The team must find pictures of at least five foods they can ALL agree upon as being ones they like. Each picture must be initialed and arranged in a collage which is then signed by all teammembers.

INDIVIDUAL ACCOUNTABILITY:
Teacher monitoring and random checking of individuals for agreement.
The initials on the pictures and signing the product.

DEBRIEFING:
- Share a food upon which your team agreed.
- What were some foods NOT found in your collage that you liked, but that the others did not agree?
- Raise your hand if you...
  Signed the collage... If you initialed at least one picture.

Teams huddle and discuss...
- What made this collage difficult to complete?
- Who in your team asked, "Does everyone agree?"
- What could your team do differently to improve?

Appreciation statement...
- Think of one thing each of your teammates did which seemed to help your team. Share this with them.

LIBRARY - MEDIA
BY Susan Bauer
Team size: 2   Time limit: 30 minutes

ACTIVITY:
The teams are asked to imagine that they are now the Media Specialist. Each team will be given a different situation about a student who comes in and wants a particular book. The groups will list the procedures that they would use to help the student find the book.

SOCIAL SKILLS: (Ground Rules)
- Quiet voices
- Take turns
- Mistakes are okay
- SIGNAL TO STOP IS:..."May I have your attention please!"

MATERIALS:
1 Paper with the instructions
1 Pencil and paper (for writing responses)
1 Team Card (with Ground Rules) for making tallies

ROLES:
Reader - reads the problem
Writer - Lists the procedures to follow to help someone find a book
Roles are switched after each problem, both help to solve the problem

GOAL:
Receive at least 4 tallies (stamps) on the Team Card
Write down the process for finding the book

INDIVIDUAL ACCOUNTABILITY:
Teacher monitoring, random checking. At a later date give students individual problems to solve to locate a book.

DEBRIEFING:
Teams stand if...
- You met the goal of receiving 4 stamps/tallies and completing the solution...

Teams Share...
- Partnered up with another team, trade your solution, each team will follow the directions from another team to confirm correctness (trying to locate the book). Three minutes to locate the book.
- In three minutes you will meet again with your Partnered Team and share how well the solution was written or any suggestions to improve the directions.

Appreciation statement...
- Share with your partner, "___, you did a good job of..."

MUSIC-APPRECIATION
BY   Ron Shields   (adapted)

Team size: 2   Time limit: 20 minutes

ACTIVITY:
Teams will place composers on a map in the country of their birthplace.

SOCIAL SKILLS: (Ground Rules)
- Quiet voices
- Take turns
- Mistakes are okay
- Reach agreement
- SIGNAL TO STOP IS: sound of tuning pipe

MATERIAL:
1 map
1 list of composers
2 pencils / pens different colors

ROLES:
Researcher- looks up the composer and country of birth.
Recorder - finds location on the map and writes composer's name.
Roles switch after locating each composer

GOAL:
Follow the Ground Rules
Locate all the Composers' birthplaces

INDIVIDUAL ACCOUNTABILITY:
Teacher monitoring and randomly checking individuals.
Test given, individually, at a later date.
Different color ink/lead.

DEBRIEFING:
Teams Share...
- Go to another team and compare locations with the composers.

Huddle with your partner...
- What made this assignment easy? Difficult?
- What did you learn by checking with another team?
- If a mistake was made during this activity - what was said?
  Who would like to share this? (ask for volunteers)
- How can I tell if you and your partner took turns?

Individually write...
- One thing you and your partner did to reach agreement.
- One thing your partner did to make the assignment easier.
  Share this with your partner. **(Appreciation statement)**

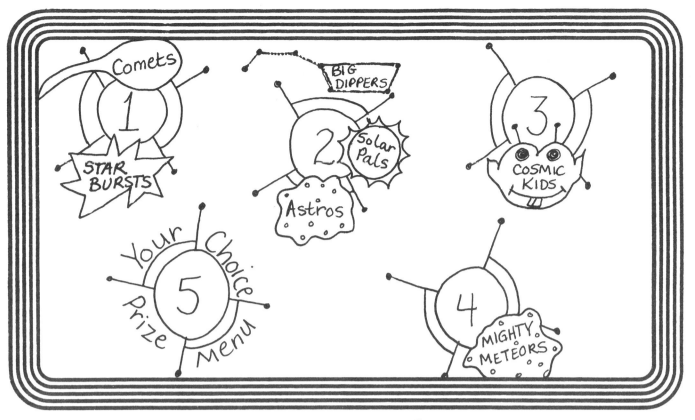

Bulletin Board - Incentive
BY: teachers at Mabel Rush School

Each team creates its own **"team name tag"** which travels around the board as the team earns bonus points, tallies, stamps, etc. When the team reaches "Satellite 5" the team members can choose a reward from the prize menu.

The board's theme changes about every 4-6 weeks. Themes could include: Space, animals, occupations, music groups, transportation, etc.

123

COOPERATIVELY...
We can do together, What many of us
Can NOT do alone...
-Teresa Cantion

Teachers have used this phrase as a bulletin board heading and had students bring pictures, clippings, sayings, etc. which deal with cooperation. Thus, students begin realizing that cooperation occurs not only in the classroom, but outside the school setting as well.

The 🔑 to SUCCESS is TEAMWORK!

"WE"
not
"I"

Share
Cooperate
Agree

"TOGETHERNESS"

BY   Joyce Givens (adapted)

Bulletin boards can also display work which the TEAM accomplished together, giving the classroom the atmosphere of a "WE" environment instead of strictly a "ME" environment.

101 ways to ENCOURAGE

Team_____ Team_____ Team_____ Team_____ Team_____
___Name_____ ___Name_____ _Name_____ _Name_____ _Name_____

BY: Susan Mobley

Teams think of all the things that they can **say** or **do** to **encourage** someone.
The teams list (in their own handwriting) under their Team Name all the ideas they
came up with to encourage others.

You're doing a great job!

TREASURES
that come from:

COOPERATION...

BY: Diana Hilton

Teams think of all the benefits of Cooperation and working in Teams. They can
put these ideas of benefits under the treasure chests.

Other ideas could include: putting pictures or magazine/newspaper articles
which illustrate or describe cooperation, under the treasure chests.

Ground Rules can also be listed as part of this bulletin board.

BIBLIOGRAPHY OF COOPERATIVE LEARNING
RESOURCES FOR EDUCATORS

Section 12

BIBLIOGRAPHY
Cooperative Learning: resources for educators

KEY to books on next page.

AIMS EDUCATION FOUNDATION :
        Write for list of books with teacher-submitted activities in Cooperative Learning strategies.
        Activiities in Math and Science. ($10.95 + 10% handling)**
ORDER FROM: P.O. Box 7766, Fresno, CA 93747

Cantlon, Teresa L.   STRUCTURING THE CLASSROOM SUCCESSFULLY FOR COOPERATIVE
    1991   TEAM LEARNING * **   ($24 includes postage, Canada add $2) Third Edition

    1991   THE FIRST FOUR WEEKS OF COOPERATIVE LEARNING, activities and
                materials * ** #   ($22 includes postage, Canada add $2)

ORDER FROM: Prestige Publishers, PO Box 19044, Portland, OR 97219

For training from Teresa Cantlon:
        C&M Education Consultants, PO Box 19044 Portland, OR 97219
        (503)588-0222   or   (503)694-5970

Dale Seymore Publications**
        Write for free catalog of materials. Many are adaptable to Cooperative Learning lessons.
ORDER FROM: P.O. Box 10888, Palto Alto, CA 94303

Dinkmeyer   ENCOURAGEMENT BOOK, THE # ($8.95 + post.)
    1980   Zephyr Press, PO Box 13448-A, Dept. 26
ORDER FROM: Tucson, AZ 85732-3448

Dishon, Dee & O'Leary, Pat Wilson
    1984   A GUIDEBOOK FOR COOPERATIVE LEARNING: A TECHNIQUE FOR CREATING
                MORE EFFECTIVE SCHOOLS   ($19.95) *
ORDER FROM: Learning Publications, Inc.
                P.O. Box 1326, Holmes Beach, Florida 33509

Glasser, William   CONTROL THEORY IN THE CLASSROOM ^ ($5.95)
    1986   Harper & Row
ORDER FROM: local book stores

Goldstein, et al   SKILL STREAMING THE ADOLESCENT #   1980
ORDER FROM: Research Press Co. (also available for elementary)

Gibbs, Jeanne   TRIBES; A PROCESS FOR SOCIAL DEVELOPMENT AND COOPERATIVE
    1987   LEARNING.   ($19.95 plus $2.25 postage)**
ORDER FROM: Center for Human Development
                3702 Mr. Diablo Blvd., Lafayette, CA 94549

Huggins, Pat   TEACHING COOPERATION SKILLS, THE ASSIST PROGRAM ($20)**#
    1986
ORDER FROM: 7024 N. Mercer Way
                Mercer Island, WA 98040   ph: (206) 232-94487

Johnson, David & Roger et al
    1986   CIRCLES OF LEARNING (revised) COOPERATION IN THE CLASSROOM
                                    ($13 inc. post)^

Johnson, David & Roger et al
1987   STRUCTURING COOPERATIVE LEARNING, LESSON PLANS FOR TEACHERS
                                        ($15 plus $3 post)**

1988   OUR COOPERATIVE CLASSROOM   ($10 plus $3 post)**#
ORDER FROM: Interaction Book Company
                7208 Cornelia Drive, Edina, MN 55435   ph: (612) 831-9500

Kagan, Spencer   COOPERATIVE LEARNING, RESOURCES FOR TEACHERS ($20)*
        1989
ORDER FROM: Resources for Teachers, suite 201
                27402 Camino Capistrano, Laguna Niguel, CA 92677

Kreidler, William   CREATIVE CONFLICT RESOLUTION   ($10.50)**#
        1984   Good Year Books
ORDER FROM: Department GYB
                1900 East Lake Avenue, Glenview, Illinois 60025

Male, Mary, et al
        1988   PARTNERSHIPS: DEVELOPING TEAMWORK AT THE COMPUTER ($20)
ORDER FROM: Educational Apple-cations
                125 Sylvar Street, Santa Cruz, CA 95060

Rhodes, Jacqueline & McCabe, Margaret
        1985   SIMPLE COOPERATION IN THE CLASSROOM, A BEGINNER'S GUIDE TO
                    ESTABLISHING COOPERATIVE GROUPS   ($17.45)*

        1988   THE NURTURING CLASSROOM   ($24+post.)**
ORDER FROM: ITA Publications
                PO Box 1599, Willits, CA 95490

Simon, Sidney   I AM LOVEABLE AND CAPABLE , IALAC -pamphlet #
                    A pamphlet written as a combatant against "put-downs."

                    PAMPHLET ($1.50 + $2 post. per order) Cat. # AC5217
                    VIDEO ($25 + $2 post) Cat.# AC547V

ORDER FROM: Social Studies School Service
                10200 Jefferson Blvd., PO Box 802
                Culver City, CA 90232-9983

Schmidt, Fran & Friedman,Alice
        1985   CREATIVE CONFLICT SOLVING FOR KIDS grades 4-9   ($13.95)**#
ORDER FROM: Peace Education Foundation, Inc.
                PO Box 19-1153, Miami Beach, FL 33139

WALKER SOCIAL SKILL CURRICULUM   ($24) #
ORDER FROM: Pro Ed, 5341 Industrial Oaks Blvd.,
                Austin, TX 78735

Frog Publications
P.O. Box 280096 Tampa, FL 33682-0096
(813) 935-5845 (800) 777-FROG

These Frog Publications materials are designed in a **fun** format, as a review of the basic skills in reading and math.

They can be used in the **Colored Card** format to review and reinforce the basic skills for elementary and special education students

Call Frog Publications' Toll Free number, **mention Teresa's name and book**.You will be sent a free sample of their materials.

Key: ˆ =theory , *= formatting, **=lessons and activities, #= social skills activities

APPENDIX

Section 13

Student Attitude Survey

Learning Preference Inventory

Lesson Plan Format

Checklist for Teacher Observation

Observer's Reference Form - Social Skill/Role "Scripts"

Reaching Agreement-Consensus

Teams Score Sheet

Debriefing Forms-half sheets

Trustbuilding-Bonding -Venn Diagram

Ground Rules -for desktops

Encourager Skill Cards

Taking Turns Skill Cards

Team Cards Formats

Folded Corners Format

Seating Arrangement

Colored Cards - commercial version

Pyramid Team Goals Idea Sheet

Passport-used like Team Card

Teacher "scripts" for Simple Structures

Socio-Gram Format Review

134

TO:

FROM: Teresa L. Cantlon

RE: Student Survey - Questionnaire

Enclosed you will find a copy of a questionnaire for students with instructions for teachers. Please feel free to copy and distribute to your teachers.

The intent of this questionnaire is to measure attitude changes in students who have been in classrooms using Cooperative Learning strategies on a regular basis.

Most ideally it could be administered prior to any Cooperative Learning involvement and administered after some Cooperative strategies had begun developing in your school or classrooms.

If Cooperative Learning strategies are already in place, or just beginning, it will be interesting to track the students' attitudes every six months, (because we believe attitudes have a direct relationship to academic achievement).

If you are interested in doing this survey, I would suggest you have all teachers administer it (at the end of first period, as an example) so you get accurate feedback regarding the students at your school.

QUESTIONNAIRE - FOR STUDENTS

DIRECTIONS TO THE TEACHER:

This is a short (1-3 minute) questionnaire designed to check attitudes of students about their learning, friendships, and school, which studies indicate have an impact on learning and students' self esteem.

The students should have a feeling that whatever they mark is **anonymous**. To set this atmosphere consider the following format:

INSTRUCTIONS TO THE STUDENTS:

This is a short questionnaire asking questions about your attitudes relating to school, which is to be done **anonymously** (without anyone knowing how you marked your answers, including the teacher).

RATIONALE:
They (the questionnaires) will be used to assist teachers in their teaching.

I will ask one (or two) of you to pass out these questionnaires. When you receive the questionnaire **carefully follow the directions**...
REMEMBER: to put your grade, age and gender (sex), but do <u>not</u> sign your name.

When finished put the questionnaire in the large envelope located...(wherever you place the envelope, on a desk, table, front of the room, etc.).

So that you understand I **will not** know how you answered these questions or which paper is yours, I will stand... (at the back of the room, outside the door, or wherever is appropriate).

Be sure you do your own questionnaire and **do not** compare answers with one another until **after** class session when you have placed your questionnaire in the envelope.

Suggestion to teacher: for your convenience, you might want to do this survey the last five minutes of a class session.

If there is a designated person in charge of the survey:

Upon completion, return to:

On or before:

Student Survey

DIRECTIONS: Do <u>NOT</u> sign your name.
Write or respond with your <u>FIRST</u> thought.

GRADE: _____

AGE: _____

FEMALE ☐   MALE ☐

Check One:

1. I ☐always ☐usually ☐never ☐sometimes enjoy school.

2. I have ☐many ☐few ☐no friends.

3. There are ☐many ☐few ☐no opportunities to make new friends in my classes.

4. The way to meet, make new friends at our school is:

Check One:

5. School is a ☐cooperative ☐competitive ☐isolated place to be.

Check one or more:

6. I learn new information best when I can... ☐see/read it ☐hear it explained ☐can actually do it ☐can explain it to someone else.

Check one:

7. I am ☐always ☐usually ☐never happy.

8. ☐Some ☐Few ☐None of my teachers have us work in small groups.

9. If yes to number 8...write in 1, 2, 3, etc. ☐ teachers have us work in groups at least twice a week.

10. I am at school because:

Learning Preferences - A Checklist - How We Learn

Name_____   date_____

Instructions:
Place a checkmark by the phrase that **BEST describes** the way you learn.

1. It is easier for me to learn...   _____ what I have read.   (v)
                                          _____ what I have heard.   (a)
                                          _____ when I make something   (tk)

2. I would rather...   _____ read a story.   (v)
                                          _____ listen to a story.   (a)
                                          _____ make a project.   (tk)

3. When working on a project I...   _____ prefer working alone   (al)
                                          _____ like to work with another person or
                                          small group.   (g)

4. I would rather...   _____ read to learn how to do something.   (v)
                                          _____ make something with hands.   (tk)
                                          _____ be told how to do something.   (a)

5. I get more work done when I...   _____ work with someone.   (g)
                                          _____ work alone.   (al)

6. When memorizing new information, I can remember best when I...
                                          _____ repeat it over and over   (a)
                                          _____ read it several times.   (v)
                                          _____ write and repeat it.   (tk)

7. I...   _____ can learn from others when
                                          working in a group.   (g)
                                          _____ am distracted by others when
                                          working in a group.   (al)

8. I remember what I have learned best, when I...
                                          _____ make things for my studies.   (tk)
                                          _____ read the material.
                                                                               (v)
                                          _____ listen to the material.   (a)

Directions- Total the number of (a)'s, (v)'s, (tk)'s, (al)'s and (g)'s and put numbers on lines below:

_____   _____   _____   _____   _____
auditory   visual   tactile/kinesth.   alone   group

Submitted by Charlotte Redfield   ©C&M EDUCATION CONSULTANTS

137

LESSON PLAN FORMAT for COOPERATIVE LEARNING
To use as a **guideline**, write on your own paper for more space.

TEAM SIZE:

TIME LIMIT for entire lesson:
TARGET TIME for Student work:

TEAM COMPOSITION: heterogeneous by...
*

ACTIVITY: lesson to be done...
*

GROUND RULE or SOCIAL SKILL (emphasized during this lesson)
*
*

The way this social skill will be emphasized is by: E.g., Going over scripts, modeling, reviewing, etc.
*

--Signal to stop is ... •
--Back-Up signal is... •
(when students are interacting and a voice is not affective)

MATERIALS: shared or limited ?
*
*

ROLES: If necessary and appropriate. If assigned, what is the responsibility of the role?.
*

GOAL+ reward = feedback:
What the TEAM must do to be successful, and how they know they have accomplished the goal-reward/feedback system.
*
*

INDIVIDUAL ACCOUNTABILITY:
How will the teacher monitor students' knowledge: random checking, post-test, etc.

*
*

DEBRIEFING: summary and closure of the lesson
List specific questions which reflect back on the lesson. To be asked after the cooperative activity. What formats will be incorporated? E.g., Thumbs Up, Partner Share, Team Stand, Team Share, Interview, etc.
*
*
*

The teacher debriefs last with specific feedback from observation data, Student Debriefing Forms, or from the Team Cards on the students' desks.

Note: remember to encourage students to include an appreciation statement (affirm one another).
E.g., *"Share with you partner ways he/she helped you today."*
Refer to: pages 95-122 for lesson plan formatting ideas

Checklist For Teacher Observation - Cooperative Learning

Teacher _____   Date of Observation: _____   Date for Return: _____
Grade/Subject: _____   Date of Conference: _____   Observer: _____

	observed YES	not observed NO	Observed / Comments:
Team size two			
Some threes			
Other:			
Composition -girl/boy			
Other:			
Room arrangement: side-by-side			
No backs to the teacher			
Partners			
Diads with partners			
Class environment says "we"			
Ground Rules posted			
Two-four rules			
Positive, short, concise			
Signal to Stop used			
Pause			
Students responded			
Lesson/Activity set-up (modeling, role playing) Directions clear:			
Checked for understanding			
Social Skill(s) included list skill(s)			
social skill taught **or**			
social skill reviewed			
social skill fit the lesson			
Goal stated(team success)			
Stated purpose/rationale of lesson			
Limited/shared materials			
Roles			
roles fit the lesson			
Target time given			
Energizers used students allowed to stand/move			
Activity while students are working together Students included equally			
Noise level appropriate			
Teacher wandering			
Monitoring/Adjusting as needed			
Giving feedback			
Signal to Stop used			
Pause			
Students responded			
Energizers used students allowed to stand/move			

Debriefing (summary closure done)
Oral (circle) Written

Format: (circle any used)
Individual   With Partner   Team Share   Interview   Other:

Teacher feedback:
Individual   Team by Team   Whole Class   Other:

Questions asked by teacher to students or teams: Write specific questions here (verbatim).

Checklist For Teacher Observation - Cooperative Learning

Check if any Simple Structures were observed, keeping everyone involved (active participation) throughout a lesson, activity, instructions or direction giving.

> **Suggestion:** Take verbatim data on the directions given by the teacher setting up these Simple Structures. Often teachers ask the students to : *"Turn to your partner,"* before they have given the students instructions on what they will be sharing with their partner.

Refer to: Simple Structures, pages 31-40

	Observed	The directions to the students, verbatim as stated by the teacher:

Partner Share

Team Share

Team Stand

Red Dot / Blue dot

Interview

Think - Write-Share

Round Robin

Jigsaw

Paraphrase

Brainstorm

Oral Choral

Folded Corners

Colored Cards

Skill Cards

Observer Skill Cards

Thumbs Up/Pens Up

Make A Date

Bag It / Box It

Corners/Line Up

Other/Comments:

Scripts for Skill Cards

When using Skill Cards, run off <u>only</u> the Script for referral by the Observer
Refer to: SIMPLE STRUCTURES - Observer/Skill Cards page 39

IDEA GIVER:

I THINK...

MAYBE...

MY IDEA IS...

WE COULD...

A WAY TO DO THIS IS...

ANOTHER WAY IS TO...

QUESTIONER:

WHAT DO YOU THINK ...?

WOULD YOU LIKE...?

WHO WOULD LIKE TO...?

WHAT'S THE BEST WAY TO...?

HOW SHOULD WE...?

WHO KNOWS...?

WHEN SHOULD WE...?

DO YOU HAVE ANY IDEAS...?

ENCOURAGER:

THAT'S A GOOD IDEA.

THAT MAKES SENSE.

I LIKE YOUR SUGGESTIONS

THAT'S IT! THAT'S REALLY GREAT!

GREAT JOB!

THANK YOU, _____!

WHAT DO YOU THINK?

YOU HAVE GOOD IDEAS!

SUMMARIZER:

MOST OF US THINK...

IT SEEMS LIKE ...

IT SOUNDS LIKE WE WANT...

SOME OF US WANT TO ...

BUT OTHERS WANT TO ...

Suggestion of steps that can be **taught** to students when teaching the social skill of Reaching Agreement or Consensus.

Everyone GIVES an idea and a REASON.
"My suggestion is... because..."

Others: LISTEN carefully to each idea.
REMARK POSITIVELY to the suggestion
"Good point!"   "I like that."

ACCEPT each idea or ADD ON to the idea.
"Your idea is good, I would like to add to it..."

OR

REJECT the IDEA and give the reason.
"This idea might NOT work because...what do you think?"

TALK over ALL options (ideas) and DISCARD any which DO NOT
fit or are not the BEST options.

DECIDE on the idea that your TEAM thinks will work BEST-
realizing, it might NOT be YOUR idea or your FIRST CHOICE.

Debriefing Forms - Half Sheet

Team Summary Form   date _____

Name of team members: _____

The Ground Rules are: _____

_____

Today's social goal is:_____

Today's academic goal is: _____

Today, everyone in our team learned:

_____

_____

Level of success with the social goal: lowest 1 - 2 - 3 - 4 - 5 highest

What we can do to improve next time:

_____

Amber Turney   © C&M EDUCATION CONSULTANTS

Summary   Sheet

Evaluation of Team:_____   Date: _____

Names:

Teammember:	Was helpful because:	Would have been more helpful if:
self:		
partner:		
Table Team Partners:		
Our team worked best at:		
Our team needed work at:		
I like teams because:		
I dislike teams because:		
Other comments:		
On the back draw a picture of your team doing its best work. Write under the picture an explanation.		

Linda McJunkin   © C&M EDUCATION CONSULTANTS

143

Debriefing Forms-Half Sheets

This form can be used by Table Teams. When Partners are doing Team Share activities with another team to form a Table Team.

TABLE TEAM SUMMARY SHEET

Names: _____ date:_____

This person took the assigned job seriously.   Name:_____

This member kept the Table Team on task.   Name:_____

This member made the others explain their answers.   Name:_____

This member made the other members feel a part of the team.   Name:_____

This member listened closely to others' comments.   Name: _____

This member helped the others with work, but didn't do it for them. Name:_____

This member improved the most during our teamwork.   Name:_____

Our Table Team can improve on:

Jim Perry (adapted)   ©C&M EDUCATION CONSULTANTS

This form is designed for the teacher or students to write in the Ground Rule(s) or Social Skill(s) which is being emphasized. The students respond in short sentences on the lines.

Names: _____ date_____

HOW DID WE DO?

RULE(S) OR BEHAVIOR(S):
1.
2.
3.

1._____

2._____

3._____

TEAMS SCORE SHEET

#1   Team   _____ _____

#2   Team   _____ _____

#3   Team   _____ _____

#4   Team   _____ _____

#5   Team   _____ _____

#6   Team   _____ _____

#7   Team   _____ _____

#8   Team   _____ _____

#9   Team   _____ _____

#10   Team   _____ _____

#11   Team   _____ _____

#12   Team   _____ _____

#13   Team   _____ _____

#14   Team   _____ _____

#15   Team   _____ _____

#16   Team   _____ _____

This sheet can be run on transparency film and used on the overhead to record teams pretest and post-test scores for the Colored Cards activity or for showing team gains. This shows the teams they are meeting their goal.

145

Name _____ Skill: Compare and contrast

A Delightfully Different Diagram

Find out how you and a partner are alike and different by using a Venn diagram (overlapping circles). Let's say you have brown hair and a dog, and your partner has red hair and a dog. Let circle **A** represent you and circle **B** represent you partner. The part where the circles overlap is called the **intersection**. This part represents what you both have in common.

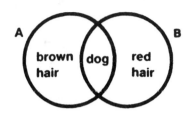

On this diagram, use the list of categories below to compare yourself with a partner.

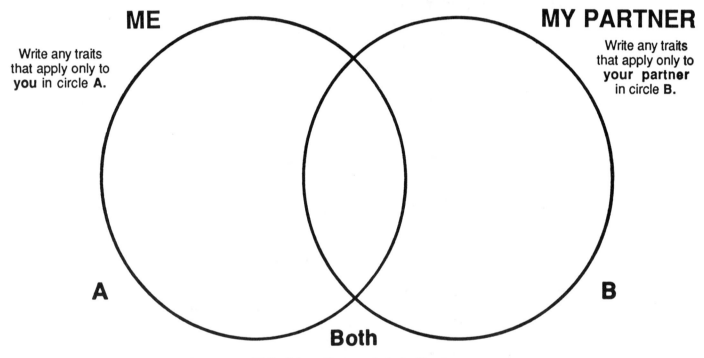

ME

Write any traits that apply only to **you** in circle **A**.

A

MY PARTNER

Write any traits that apply only to **your partner** in circle **B**.

B

Both

Write things that apply to **both of you** in the **intersection** of the circles.

Physical Traits
- ☐ hair and eye color
- ☐ height
- ☐ weight
- ☐ age
- ☐ _____

Personality Traits
- ☐ shy/outgoing
- ☐ serious/silly
- ☐ quiet/talkative
- ☐ daring/cautious
- ☐ _____

Social Traits
- ☐ clubs
- ☐ sports
- ☐ activities
- ☐ hobbies
- ☐ _____

Statistics
- ☐ number in family
- ☐ times moved
- ☐ number of pets
- ☐ languages spoken
- ☐ _____

Preferences
- ☐ favorite subject
- ☐ favorite food
- ☐ color (likes/dislikes)
- ☐ free time use
- ☐ _____

(Other)
- ☐ talents
- ☐ _____
- ☐ _____
- ☐ _____
- ☐ _____

146

Submitted by Judy Ramstead, resource unkno

···si dots ot ɹɐubıs-

-mistakes are okay

-take turns

-quiet voices

GROUND RULES

--run on heavy paper----------------------fold here---------------------place on team desks--

GROUND RULES

-quiet voices-

-take turns-

-mistakes are okay-

-signal to stop is...-

147

GROUND RULES

-12 inch voices

-contribute ideas

-stay on task

-listen to others

-signal to stop is...

--run on heavy paper----------------------fold here-------------------------place on team desks--

GROUND RULES

-12 inch voices

-contribute ideas

-stay on task

-listen to others

-signal to stop is..

148

GROUND RULES

-stay with your team

-try ideas

-quiet voices

-ask the teacher ONLY if you ALL have
the same question

-signal to stop is...   149

--run on heavy paper----------------------fold here--------------------------place on team desks--

GROUND RULES

-stay with your team

-try ideas

-quiet voices

-ask the teacher ONLY if you ALL have
the same question

-signal to stop is...

DIRECTIONS: Cut these into small cards, flashcard format. Put the pile between the teammembers. Each time an encouragement is given, by a partner, they receive an Encourager card.
Debrief: After the activity, partners can share with one another how they received the cards and what was said. They can go to another team and Team Share "scripts" which they used to receive their Encourager Cards.

Encourager	Encourager
Encourager	Encourager
Encourager	Encourager
Encourager	Encourager
Encourager	Encourager
Encourager	Encourager
Encourager	Encourager
Encourager	Encourager
Encourager	Encourager
Encourager	Encourager
Encourager	Encourager
Encourager	Encourager
Encourager	Encourager

DIRECTIONS: Cut these into small cards, flashcard format. Put the pile between the teammembers. Each time a student takes a turn they take a card.

Debrief: After the activity, partners can share with one another how many cards they received, if it was equal to their partner. What they can do next activity to ensure equal participation. They can go to another team and Team Share their results and ways they took turns and what they might do differently. next time.

Taking turns	Taking turns
Taking turns	Taking turns
Taking turns	Taking turns
Taking turns	Taking turns
Taking turns	Taking turns
Taking turns	Taking turns
Taking turns	Taking turns
Taking turns	Taking turns
Taking turns	Taking turns
Taking turns	Taking turns
Taking turns	Taking turns
Taking turns	Taking turns
Taking turns	Taking turns

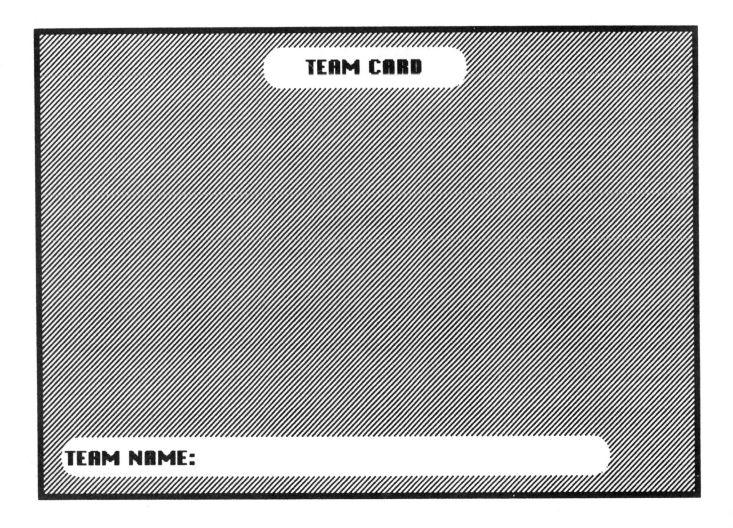

TEAM CARD

TEAM NAME:

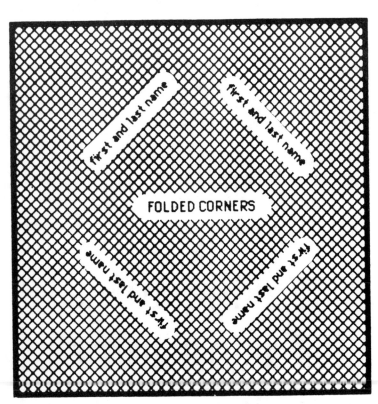

first and last name

first and last name

FOLDED CORNERS

first and last name

first and last name

Example of Team Card:
Team Cards can be index cards, pieces of paper, a Team File Folder, (with team work inside), the worksheet itself or whatever fits for giving **feedback**.

Folded Corners Card:
refer to:
Simple Structures-
Folded Corners Card

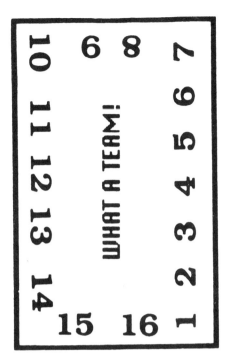

WHAT A TEAM!

6 8 7
10 11 12 13 14 9 6 5 4 3
15 16 1 2

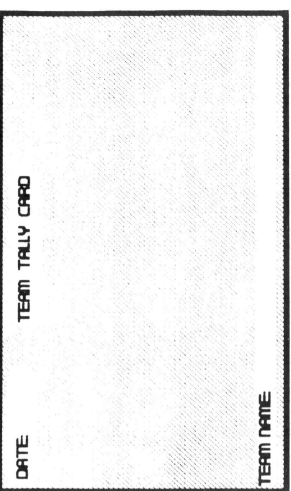

TEAM TALLY CARD

DATE

TEAM NAME

TEAM:

Quiet voices:

Taking turns:

Encouraging/praising:

Sharing ideas:

Stopping with the signal:

Finished product:

Homework:

OTHER:

Examples of Team Cards:

Team Tally Card- can be used to award tallies, stamps (with an inked stamp), apply stickers or whatever is appropriate.

The Punch Card can be punched with a hole punch. (By the way, hole punches come in assorted shapes: stars, animals, flowers, etc. They can be found at stores that sell novelty cards and paper).

The Punch Card can have X's placed over the numerals as well. When the card is filled, the team has accomplished its goal. Their card can be placed on the Pyramid board. (Example on next page). Just being on the Pyramid Board might be reward enough for the team. Or, if they make the Pyramid Board they can earn...(a privilege, grab bag items, a free drawing, etc.) Each time they fill a Punch Card the next card puts them higher on the Pyramid.

The Team Skill Card with the Skills listed is so the teacher does not have to interupt the team by verbalizing what was observed. This can be used later when teams are working well together. Initially, it is important for the students to "hear" specfic examples and feedback.
Team Skill Card idea submitted by Linda Timmel

Effective Classroom Arrangements
Especially for secondary

In addition to **Square Horseshoe:** (page 155)

Partners in Rows (staggered Rows)

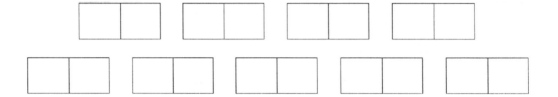

Three/Four Rows - gentle "U"

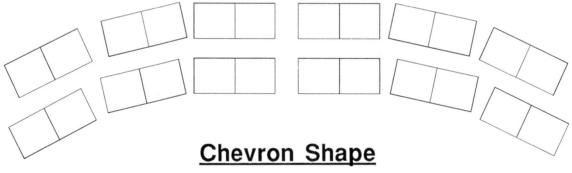

Chevron Shape

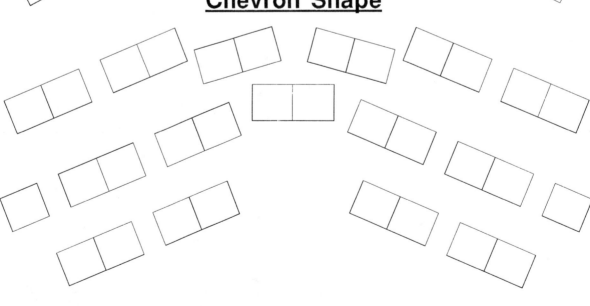

Seating Arrangement

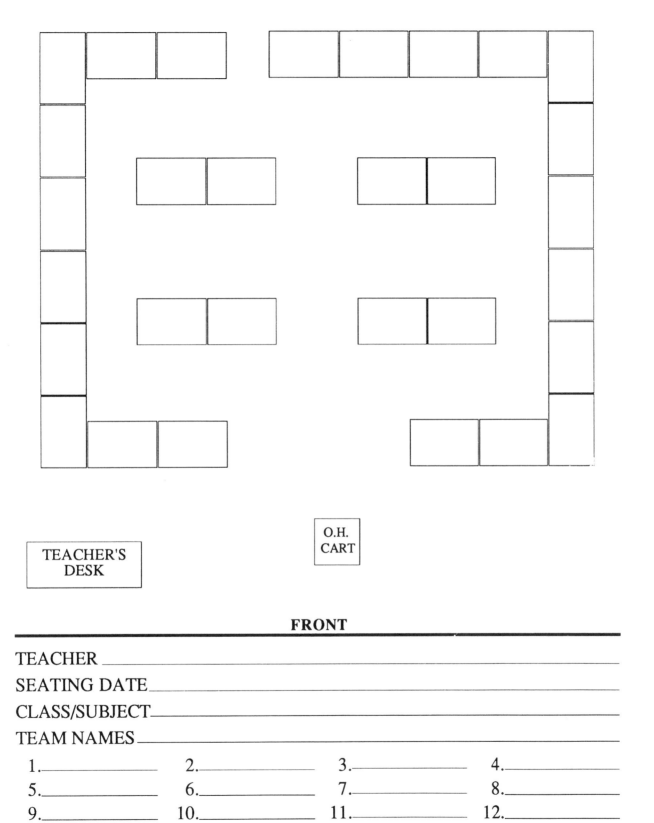

TEACHER'S DESK

O.H. CART

FRONT

TEACHER _____

SEATING DATE _____

CLASS/SUBJECT _____

TEAM NAMES _____

1._____ 2._____ 3._____ 4._____

5._____ 6._____ 7._____ 8._____

9._____ 10._____ 11._____ 12._____

13._____ 14._____ 15._____ 16._____

Reading and Language Mastery Kits

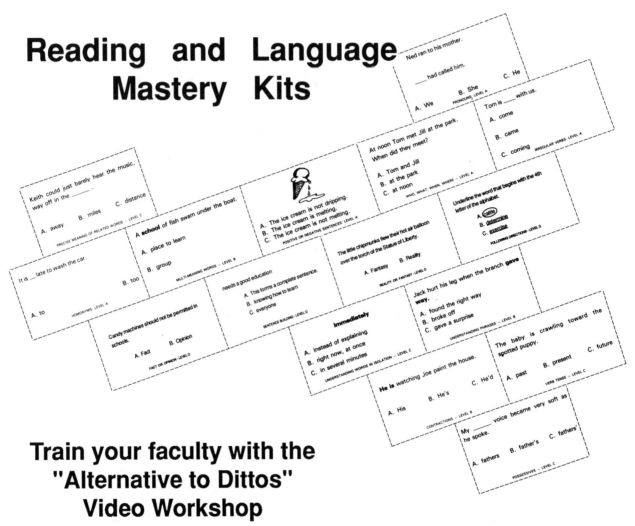

Train your faculty with the "Alternative to Dittos" Video Workshop

Your entire faculty can learn to use the practical, effective Frog System by participating in Frog Publications' 60 minute, hands-on video workshop. The video workshop will inspire and instruct as you work along with the video using skillcards and gameboards included with the video package. The complete video package is available to schools at no charge when the principal calls in the request.

I love it! This idea is easily implemented, reasonably inexpensive, and very versatile!
Mary Muffott
Sterling Park Elementary
Casselberry, FL

Super idea to motivate kids to learn!
Bonnie Brook
A. C. Perry Elementary
Cooper City, FL

CALL TOLL-FREE (800) 777-FROG (3764)

Each Kit Contains

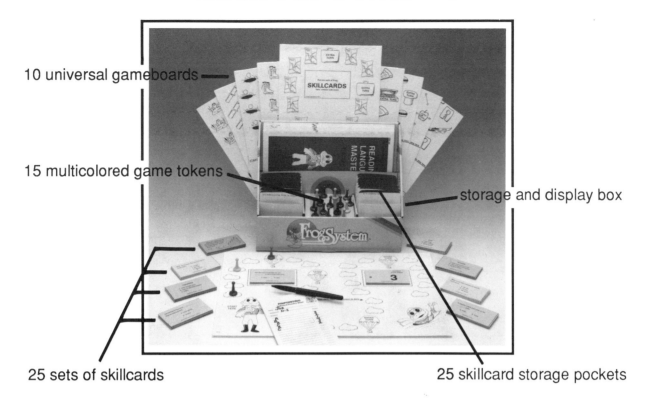

10 universal gameboards

15 multicolored game tokens

storage and display box

25 sets of skillcards

25 skillcard storage pockets

Readiness Concepts Kit

Requires no reading but a lot of thinking.
For kindergarten and first grade.

Level A Kit

For any child reading independently in the range of 1.5 - 2.5.

Level B Kit

For any child reading independently in the range of 2.0 - 3.5.

Level C Kit

For any child reading independently in the range of 3.0 - 4.5.

Level D Kit

For any child reading independently in the range of 4.0 - 5.5.

Additional materials in reading and math also available.

After your workshop we implemented the complete Frog System schoolwide. It has proven to be a most worthwhile investment!
Peg McCaughey, Principal
Thomas Jefferson Elementary
Jacksonville, FL

Use these well-done materials in the Colored Cards format to reinforce reading and math skills. With students "teaching" one another and learning these much needed skills in a "game-like" format.

PYRAMID TEAM GOALS

ALL TEAMS CLASS GOAL

Earns_____

100

Earns_____

80

Earns_____

60

Earns_____

20

Earns_____

40

Earns_____

Example for students to monitor their goals.

This can be done team by team as well as class goal setting.

One idea is to fill a team Punch Card and put the Card on the 20, when the second is filled, it goes on the 40, etc.

Another idea could be when a team earns 20 tallies (or any numbers can be placed on the Pyramid), stamps, etc. their name goes on the 20. The next twenty they earn their team name goes on the 40, etc.

Still another idea might be: the total of the teams' class tallies for the day goes on the Pyramid until the class reaches the top!

1 _____ 2 _____

3 _____ 4 _____

5 _____

PASSPORT

PASSPORT: Anne LaVietes (adapted)

Use like a Team Card. Fold into fourths.
Points/tallies can be recorded on the lines in
each sqaure (day). If _X_ number are earned in a
day then the "team" Passport can be "stamped"
like a passport or a sticker placed in the square of
the day.

NAMES: _____

> A teacher "script" can **cut down direction-giving.** Scripts can often include a **social skill** into the directions and give each partner a role/responsibility with short, concise verbage. Using the **same "script"** will help students become familiar with the Simple Structure and later the teacher will only have to say, *"Do this next activity in Round Robin format, red-dot is the reader, blue dot the encourager, switch roles after three questions."* Note:Short consice directions, social skills of taking turns and enouraging are built into the script.

SUGGESTION: Put each Simple Structure "Script" on a 5X8 card and each time you want to do that activity READ the script to the teams until you are comfortable with the format and develop your own.

Partner Share: (keeps everyone actively involved)

"Everyone think about..." (the answer a posed question, etc.)
Pause, (count 10-30 alligators)
(Give 10-45 seconds "think" time-dependent on the difficulty of the question. do not look at the students during "think" time or they might stop thinking and try to be called upon)

"Both partners will share their ideas, start with the ...partner"
(Partner on the left/right or blue dot/red dot, etc.)

Team Stand:
(keeps everyone actively involved, checks for understanding and is an energizer)

"Everyone think about..." (the answer a posed question, etc.)
Pause (Count 10-45 alligators)
(Give 10-45 seconds "think" time-dependent on the difficulty of the question. Do not look at the students during "think" time or they might stop thinking and try to be called upon.

"When I say, 'go' both partners will share their ideas, start with the partner on the ... (left/right or blue dot/red dot, etc.). **Go!"**

"Everyone's attention..."
Pause (count 7-10 alligators)

"When I day 'go' decide with your partner on one answer/idea and stand quietly when you have that answer/idea." *"Go!"*

"One team standing...two teams...five teams, etc., all teams standing."

"I will now point to a team, together, you and your partner share aloud your idea/answer, after you have shared your idea/answer your team may be seated, if any other team had a similar idea/answer you may be seated also." (begin pointing to partner teams)

Think, Write, Share:
(keeps everyone actively involved and a means for checking for understanding)

"Think about the answer to..."

Pause 10-45 seconds (depending on level of difficulty).

"Write down the answer you came up with." **Pause** (allowing time to write)

"When I say 'go' you will share your answer with your partner. If you have the same answer as your partner put your thumb/pencil up. If you do not have the same answer discuss your reason for your answer."

"Starting with the partner on the (left/right or blue dot/red dot) share your answer"

"Go"

Oral Choral: (keeps all students actively involved, a means for checking under-standing-if an incorrect answer is heard clarification/adjustment may be done)

"Think about the answer to ..."

Pause 10-45 seconds depending on level of difficulty.

"Everyone, what is the answer?" (everyone responds aloud)

Or:

"Think about the directions to the next activity." **PAUSE**

Partners on the left (blue dot) what do you do? Everyone?"

"Partners on the right (red dot) what is your job?"

"Everyone, how many papers are you to use?"

"Everyone, how much time do you have to do this assignment?"

Round Robin: (keeps everyone involved, incorporates the social skills of taking turns and encouragement. -a script to avoid "put-downs".)

"Using one paper and different colored writing instruments:

Partner on the left (red dot) *does the first _____ and records* (writes).

Partner on the right (blue dot) *assists and gives encouragement such as: 'Good job'* or *'I agree!'*

Next _(problem, answer, etc.)_ partner on the right (blue dot)records (writes) and partner on the left (red dot) assists and gives encouragers."

Corners: (energizer, class bonding, checking with other than own partner, gain new ideas, incorporate the social skills of coming to agreement (consensus) and accepting another's opinion, giving reason and rationale.)

Various ways to do Corners-

Option I
"When you finish your assignment stand. Look around for the next person that stands. This will be your 'checking partner.'
 (If done as partners, they will stand and check with another partner team).

Go to a corner (or side of the room together) and compare your answers.

If you agree on all answers both of you sign both papers.

If you do NOT agree on answer redo the problem by saying 'I think the answer is _____ BECAUSE_____'

*If you agree with the new answer write it in and put a * by that answer.*

*If you can NOT come to agreement on an answer put two** (stars) by that answer."*

(Teacher checks for understanding here and/or has the directions/steps on the chalkboard, overhead or on a piece of paper for the the students to reference.)

Corners:

Option II

"Those of you who do not understand _____ go to this corner and John and Lisa will go through the steps with you. Remember, after you learn the steps you must explain them to someone else in your corner."

"Those of you who do not understand _____ go to that corner and Byron and Jennifer will go through the steps with you. Remember, after you learn the steps you must explain them to someone else in your corner."

NOTE: Establish as many stations (corners) as necessary with appropriate amount of student tutors to give assistance and feedback. The assistants are responsible for making sure everyone in their "Corner" understands and can explain or give reason and rationale for their answer. They are NOT giving answers but rather interpreting and "teaching" in their own words.

Other "Corners" Options: Whenever you want students to share ideas, information, check answers or interpret information they can go to a designated corner or specified part of the room, find a new partner or go as a team and Team Share with a new team their findings.

Author's suggestion: Take 1 copy of pages160-163 cut apart and affix on 5X8 inch cards. When initially implementing the Simple Structures "read" these scripts as the directions for the cooperative activity until you become comfortable and confident with the vocabulary. Then use your own words and cut down the directions even more!

Socio-Gram Example: Review

For higher level of success in getting a more diverse distribution of scores increase the number of options.

E.g., *"List 5 students from this class whom you would like on your _____ team."*

Or: *"Write down the name of a boy from this class you would like to go to the _____ with."*

"Write the name of a girl from this class that you would like to share a _____ with."

Ask questions until students have 4-5 classmates listed.

For younger students who have difficulty writing ask them to circle pictures from a class picture or individually tell the teacher **4-5** choices of classmates.

Tally the number of votes each student receives and put the list into girl/boy columns in heirarchy of votes received. Highest number on top.

> **NOTE:** Put a student from **above** the line with a student from **below** the line of the opposite gender. Make sure there is **at least** a 3 point spread with a 0 (no less, but **much higher spread** is preferable) and **at least** a two point spread with all other numbers.

If you must make a threesome, due to odd number in the class, place **two higher numbers with one low**. This way the two highs model for the low. If the opposite occurs, (two lows with a high) there is often the modeling of inappropriate behavior. **Divide your students** fifty percent girls and fifty percent boys if possible unless too many 0's, 1's, and 2's fall in one gender or the other.

> **Directions:** Using the following names divide this list in half, (half the low numbers above the line and half below regardless of gender) and draw lines placing someone above the 50% line with someone below the line. Keep in mind that 0's must go with **at least 3 or higher** and all other numbers must have **at least a two point spread**, but place with higher spread if possible or workable.

BOYS	GIRLS
John 9	Shannon 8
Bob 6	Rebecca 6
Phil 5	Cassie 5
Dick 4	Brenda 5
Braden 4	Jennifer 5
Brad 4	Tami 4
Dale 3	Laurie 4
Calvin3	Teri 3
Adam 2	Sara 1
Eugene 1	
Cameran 1	
Joe 0	

Reminder: mixed gender is important, but **secondary** to social skills.
Check next page for **one option** for teaming from this socio-gram.

Directions: Using the following names divide this list in half, (half the low numbers above the line and half below regardless of gender) and draw lines placing someone above the 50% line with someone below the line. Keep in mind that 0's must go with **at least 3 or higher** and all other numbers must have **at least a two point spread** but place with higher spread if possible or workable.

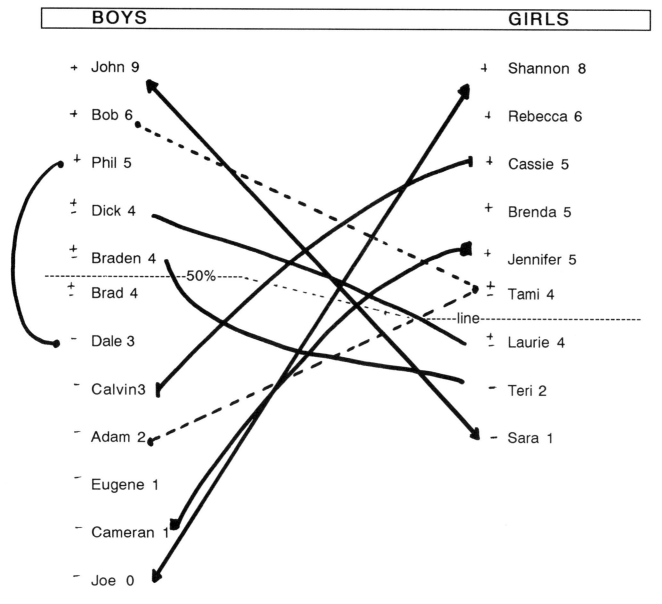

BOYS	GIRLS

+ John 9

+ Bob 6

+ Phil 5

⁺⁻ Dick 4

⁺⁻ Braden 4

--------50%-----

⁺⁻ Brad 4

⁻ Dale 3

⁻ Calvin 3

⁻ Adam 2

⁻ Eugene 1

⁻ Cameran 1

⁻ Joe 0

⁺ Shannon 8

⁺ Rebecca 6

⁺ Cassie 5

⁺ Brenda 5

⁺ Jennifer 5

⁺⁻ Tami 4

-----line--------------------------

⁺⁻ Laurie 4

⁻ Teri 2

⁻ Sara 1

You are trying to put together the most successful teams as possible. Begin with partnering the zeros, then the threesome, same-gender, and then the remainder of the class put into partnerships. Beginning with the partnering in this order is the order of the teams which often have the most difficulty. Therefore, you are making these teams as strong as possible initially. Starting with strong teams sets the tone for future teamwork and classroom management.

Reminder: mixed gender is important, but **secondary** to social skills. Some teams may have same gender for higher social skill benefits.

Threesomes are tricky. **Do not** put 0's and 1's in a threesome. Their social skills are too low. They could be left out or become a discipline problem. 6,4,2 and 7, 5, 3 are good threesome combinations. Two boys and one girl make the strongest threesome. Threesomes should always be seated at the front of the class as well as same-gender teams. These teams often need close teacher supervision.

AUTHOR'S GLOSSARY of TERMS and INDEX

Section 14

Author's Glossary of Terms and Index

Author's Glossory of Terms and Index

Author's Glossary of Terms and Index

Partners: Two students (possibly some threesomes).

Partner Share: In teams of two, turning to a partner, sharing an idea. 34

Participation Chips: Anything moveable. Chips of paper, paper clips, etc. 37

Pause: After the auditory Signal to Stop. A long pause until every team is quiet and listening. Allows students to "shift gears."14

Pivotal Position: The area where the teacher does most of his/her teaching. 7

Positive Praising: The teacher (or parents) give positive feedback to others. 18

Purpose: The reason or rationale. 12, 20, 21, 22, 69

Quiz, Exit: Given during debriefing to check individual accountability. Checking what a student learned while working on a team. 44, 52, 86

Random: Choosing teams by random selection, not setting criteria for team composition. 7

Rationale: The purpose or reason. 12, 20-22, 69

Rebond(ing): After team members have been separated by time or seating arrangement, they need to rebuild their trust with one another.

Reward: When the teacher praises, awards- tallies, bonus points,- stickers,- stamps-, etc. This is the feedback given to the team for working toward the stated goal. 51-53, 154

Role: A job to do during the cooperative activity to keep the student involved and included. 54-57, 70

Round Robin: Taking turns, writing, reading, researching, etc.. Using limited materials, sharing ideas and/or materials back and forth. 34

Script(s): Statements that partners say to one another while working. 39, 141 Or: teacher's directions to students 160-163

Shared Materials: Limited materials between partners. 43, 76

Signal to Stop: An "auditory" signal given by the teacher to get everyone's attention. 14-16, 69

Simple Structures: Those Cooperative Structures which keep students actively involved. 33-40

Skill Cards: Cards which have a social skill written on them. This card is awarded to a student when the skill is observed. 39, 150-151

Social Objective: The social skill which fits the lesson and will be monitored during the lesson.

Author's Glossary of Terms and Index

Social skills: Observable behaviors which assist the teams in working together. After the Ground rules are in place, additional social skills behaviors are added, one by one, as appropriate and needed. 14, 15, 43, 48, 49, 68

Socio-gram: Way to team by social skills and gender 8, 164

Stamp(s): Inked stamps to stamp logos or shapes on team cards. 18

Synergy: More heads together, sharing thoughts, produces more ideas.

Tally: A mark given by the teacher, giving feedback for behavior (academic or social), on the Team Card. 18

Tally Card: The teacher affixes tallies, stamps, stickers, etc. to this card. Synonymous with Team Card. 64, 152, 153

Target time: A time assigned to complete a task, additional time may be added as necessary or needed. 16, 70

Teams: Two students (possibly some threesomes).

Team Card: A card, file holder, etc. on which the teacher affixes tallies, bonus points, stamps, stickers, etc. 64, 152, 153

Team Composition: Criteria of how team members are partnered, (academic, gender, learning styles etc.). 7-10

Team Share: Two teams sharing information. With your partner, share with another team. 35, 71

Team Stand: Teams reach quick consensus and then stand. 35, 71

Team Size: Teams of two. 6

Teams of Two: Ideal team size. 6

Trustbuilding: Bonding, building trust between teammembers. 7, 13-14, 27-29, 68

Twelve-inch Voice: Quiet voice. Students need to be this close together to constitute a quiet voice.

Value Adding (Adder): Accepting someone's idea or opinion, and additional information or ideas to the original. 39

Verbatim: Word for word. 18, 44, 90

Vision Statements: Testimonials of positive statements regarding beliefs in cooperative learning.

Write/Share: After a question is asked, students think about it, write their answer, and share it with their partner, teacher, or team. 35